THE ANATOMY OF SOCIETY

THE ANATOMY OF SOCIETY

BY

GILBERT CANNAN

AUTHOR OF

"ROUND THE CORNER," "THE STUCCO HOUSE," "MENDEL," ETC.

NEW YORK

E. P. DUTTON & COMPANY

681 FIFTH AVENUE

Printed in the United States of America

CONTENTS

I

DEFINITIONS

I

DEFINITIONS

As it has been the grim privilege of those who have eyes to see to behold human life flayed by the tragedy of the European War of 1914-18, it is no less than their duty to set down what they have seen for those who shall come after them, that they may provide for their tragedies not to be as futile and sterile as this has been. Properly instructed, they should be able to protect themselves against the operation of theories so antiquated that they have lost all relation to the common practice of human existence.

It is the aim of the writer to avoid as far as possible the ideal theories which govern to so large an extent the efforts of revolutionaries, and to discover what, in fact, the organisation of society is, where it fails, and why it produces that feeling of helplessness in reaction against which men hurl themselves in the vain efforts of war and revolution, both of which apparently do but aggravate injustice and increase the inertia to which most social calamities can be traced.

There are times when young men must attempt to say what old men cannot think, and this is one of them. For old men ideas become words, and only those ideas are valid as a motive force for a change of spirit, which have not yet found expression, and are still part of that mysterious being in humanity which almost imperceptibly produces the variations of habit whereby progress is made.

The tragedy through which we have passed has made us for a little while conscious of being human, and the fate of the twentieth century depends upon our having the force necessary to maintain that consciousness long enough to undo the harm wrought by the conventionalism of the nineteenth century. Fundamentally, men, and the institutions by which they live, do not and cannot change. What can and must be altered is the relationship between men and their institutions, and the change can best be wrought by definition. That is not so simple, because human indolence has been such that thought has become painful, and the development of social machinery has reached such a pitch that life on its material side can be lived without thought. On the other hand, without thought, life on its spiritual side remains stagnant and the profoundest need of human nature turns into a bitter dissatisfaction. Hence the false exaltation with which great calamities are greeted, and hence, also, the acute disappointment which follows when those calamities are revealed as calamities and nothing more. Such disappointment is followed by a sullen creeping back into old habits, and a dull and sceptical refusal to believe in the promises of religion and art, both of which have reiterated "The kingdom of God is within you" to men who, captive in their institutions, have looked to them to realise both the kingdom and the truth of the saying. The Church, the State, the family, have all promised realisation, but all have only established tyranny because the unthinking mind has accepted them and not the truth they promised as objects of worship. It is only when the mind begins to see the visible as a symbol of the invisible that it can perceive truth at all. The science to which the honest endeavour of the nineteenth century was given was a testing of symbols, so many of which have been proved worthless as to induce the despair upon which disaster could creep with full warning but unresisted, rather welcomed. Without worship the human mind cannot endure its own success. Self-worship it loathes as the most potent deterrent upon its activity. If the worship of human nature is directed upon unworthy symbols it will, in time, so heartily detest them that it will accept any means, however vile, of destroying them.

It is easier to destroy than to build, and, therefore, men are joined together most easily for purposes of destruction, and it is such purposes that dominate the existing social machinery out of which the attempt is now being made to evolve some kind of international organisation. These purposes are more awful than worshipful, but, for lack of definition, none others are forthcoming, and it is sought to restore order to the present chaos by creating an international destructive force which shall be irresistible. Such a force can only be valid if the human capacity for worship is directed upon it; but such a force can only be detestable to that capacity, and in the end means will be found to destroy it. Such means are already being discussed by those who look to syndicalism violently to repair the injustice that violence has produced through the ages.

We have to begin at the beginning, and to attempt to achieve by taking thought what material and mechanical organisation has failed to do. Denunciation helps no one, and bitterness is barren. The machinery which feeds and clothes the many is in the hands of the few, who, carried by the impetus of ancient tradition, see the advantage of all in their own. The unthinking revolt of the many disquiets but does not enlighten them who think it right to do what they have the power to do.

This introduces the vital question: By what authority?

The hastiest examination of the social problem reveals the fact that ancient authority is broken. The symbols by which it ruled have been tested and found worthless. In old times the few and the many were agreed that there was a God from Whom all blessings and all evils flowed. As to the nature and existence of God there were schisms and divisions, but this direct and controlling interest in the affairs of men was not disputed. That God could move in a more mysterious way than men could imagine was not suspected. Those customs which survived from age to age were held to have His blessing, and those powers which could sustain themselves were accepted as having His authority, so much so, indeed, that the means of sustaining power, which do not vary from age to age, were never questioned until increasing knowledge forced upon men the need for definition. Then began—after Galileo and his revelation of the comparative unimportance of Man—the slow disintegration of human institutions which has reached its tragic climax at the beginning of the twentieth century. As this disintegration has proceeded, men, merely to live from day to day, have been forced back upon money, the symbol of work done, and, as that also has been consumed, upon credit, and finally upon labour. The organisation of credit has sufficed to pull humanity through its final tragedy, but, as that collapses, we shall have to fall back upon the organisation of labour, which is practically non-existent and cannot come into being until authority is restored to its place in the human mind.

In the first place, let it be agreed that it is

not enough for humanity collectively to live from day to day. The individual sustained by the organised work of humanity, in which he plays so infinitesimal a part, can do that for the brief period of his years, but humanity, whose existence is incalculable, cannot, because that existence is sustained by the awful processes of the universe. The individual living from day to day exists in the bubble of his own egoism, and until now humanity has emulated that pathetic example, being misled by the long line of egoists who have been set up as kings, princes and governors. Through these egoists it has been attempted to set up an authority supported by taboos, conventions and superstitions, all of which have been swept away by the intellectual effort of the nineteenth century, which proved that men were not governed by authority but by economic power which has never yet been allied with justice. The development of machinery increased economic power an hundredfold, until its influence was felt and recognised in every household, and the lack of justice in its employment has brought bitterness and despair into the great majority of human lives.

In that realisation the European War has

been only an incident in which a certain amount of social machinery has been scrapped. The top-hamper of society has been blown away and left in ruins in the mud of Flanders and Poland, the two cockpits in which the Europeans are accustomed to wrestle with their discomforts. We are not here concerned with the war, but with those great movements of the human spirit which are discernible through the smoke-clouds of the ruins it has left. Nor are we concerned with the League of Nations or Bolshevism or Socialism, or any of the catch-phrases with which modern men and women are accustomed to avoid the travail of thought. Our business is to discover, if we can, the large facts upon which thought must be based, and from them to set our minds working, if only to encourage mental activity, the only means by which the many can disconcert the few, with whom our quarrel is, not that they are few but that they are the wrong few. The fatal flaw of the present organisation of society is that it raises into positions of control the wrong type of mind, and where foresight and imagination are needed provides cupidity, cunning, a narrow traditionalism, and in a dangerous and terrible world a mean hunger for safety, to be procured with the minimum of risk. This produces the curious inversion whereby property is regarded as of more value than life. It is true, of course, that the accumulation of work done must be jealously safeguarded to facilitate the doing of work in the future, but at least an equal care should be taken for those who are to do the work. The airiest and most utopian schemes to procure security cannot do away with the fact that there will always be rough and dirty work to be done in the world. The question is: Need those who do that work be so rough and dirty as to induce a habit of mind which regards them as of no account? There lies the rub, and no tinkering with the superstructure of society can alter it. In political thinking it is usually forgotten, even by men like Cobden and Bright, and it needs a Lassalle, a Marx, a Cobbett to bring it home. Humanity is one, and an injury to one member is an injury to the whole. We have travelled far since it was admitted that the peasant described so terribly by La Bruyère was also a human being, but we have not yet so arranged matters that he can live a human life; and his slow loss of humanity as he drags through existence is a dead weight upon the advancement of the race, and those who gather up the wealth created by the millions of peasants and artisans are, by that also, condemned to a slow loss of humanity, since the weight they carry is too heavy for human shoulders. That wealth accumulated about a Prince could be borne, since he was sustained by his people, but, accumulated about an irresponsible capitalist, sustained only by his shareholders, it becomes as destructive as the lack of wealth is to those who labour at his bidding. Responsibility can only be restored by the discovery of authority, and for that we have to look to humanity, through and beyond it. That we have always done, but with eyes only lit by the sun. It is when the inward light of the soul mingles with that of the sun that the objects of every day can be seen as visions, and it is only when things are so seen that men can begin to speak the truth that is in them. Otherwise they do but repeat what has been said, or, worse still, they say that which their hearers wish to hear and become flatterers. The flatterers of a Prince were never so injurious as those of what we are pleased for the moment to call democracy.

The need of this time (as of all times) is vision, and never was there so much organised effort to crush it out of existence. So great is this effort that men are forced each in solitude to gaze in upon his own soul, thus to acquire a new blindness which prevents his seeing the great soul of humanity or the soul of the past in the handiwork of his fellows, or the soul that is in the things of Nature, birds and beasts, flowers and streams, mountains and clouds. This may be necessary. A man must be aware of his own soul before he can perceive any other, and the brooding that fills the world with silence may be the sign of pregnancy. We make a great din, the noise of many battles, the whir of many machines thrumming on land and sea and in the air, to hide this silence from ourselves, but in vain. It fills our minds with awe and anguish. It is not, we know, the silence of that peace which passes understanding. Between that and ourselves there should be the song of the human heart, but the heart is dumb and the tongue chatters without meaning, and we know, rich and poor alike, that our state is pitiful. In our desperate effort to break the silence that oppresses us we have thrown away our superfluity and are astonished that the ruin we half-desired has not come upon us. We have wasted young and vigorous men, but those who were left have been able to do the necessary work of the world, and only stupidity and greedy nationalism inflicts starvation upon certain segregated communities. Work by itself, sacrifice by itself, cannot then break the silence. Blind effort cannot undo our misery, nor can those drugs with which we alleviate our misery—dishonest words, false worship, bad art and blatant politics—much longer retain their potency. The silence before the storm is broken by the storm, but the silence which comes after it is broken by the stirring of life, the glad expansion of leaves, the chirp of insects in the grass, the crisping of the grass itself, the delighted song of birds. Such a stirring must come in the human world if we are not to perish of our own ingenuity. Subtle and cunning we may be to fill our bellies and to clothe our backs, but to fill our souls and to clothe them in the raiment of joy we have to be simple, devout and thankful.

Who, then, will break the silence? The teachers of religion mutter old incantations, the politicians consult with the financiers and cover their operations with words, but only from the hearts of the people can the great song come for which the human soul is aching with impatience. But the people are divided; their eyes gaze inward; they see nothing; they are allowed to know nothing. The impulse with which they threw themselves into the orgy of destruction is denied when it comes to building anew, because the fabric is already designed without reference to their wishes or their needs, but only with a view to the profit it can be made to yield. The society of the future, world-embracing, has been designed, or rather improvised, on the model of those hideous towns wherein all over the world the song of the human heart has been lost in the droning of machinery. Call it what you will, League of Nations, Society of Nations, International, society has taken shape as a collection of nations, each of which is a suburb of the central small city which is called Finance. Life, from being urban has become suburban, and has lost its character and its savour. That much every man can know from his own existence. It is harder for every man to know what it is that is squeezing his existence dry and at the same time giving him no joy nor beauty in which to find compensation in worship such as was vouchsafed to the feudal peasant, the splendour of whose Lord or King was as that of the sun. The suburban modern worker can find little to ease him in the report of the stale pleasures of the city of Finance, which is given to him by his illustrated paper. He must begin to ask what is done with his work that it brings him so little gain, material or spiritual, and it is not enough for him to learn that his work is gradually opening up oil-fields in Persia, mines in Canada, or wheatlands in Siberia. These names also have lost the magic of remoteness; discovery, even of Arctic regions, has become so cut and dried that he desires new romance, and turns to the Eldorado within himself and begins to ask that his daily toil shall open and dig out the treasure *there*. Here, he knows, is the true gold, but his life is governed by men who can only see the gold that is dug out of the earth, whose vastness overwhelms them so that they are filled with the earth's cruelty; and always when it comes, as in every adventure it does come, to a choice between the gold of the heart and the gold of the earth, choose the latter. It is this choice, perpetually made, that brings its perpetual retribution in which the innocent suffer with the guilty. Men pay for their greed in the stifling of their song, without which everything they do reacts to their hurt because it is not well done, and when it is done, as it is in the modern world, on a vast scale, it is hard to see whether it is done well or ill. Reaction is slow and is spread over innumerable lives, and may not come to a crisis for a generation or two. Hence the recklessness and the impudent levity with which, in the city of Finance, life for the suburbs is ordered. A law passed hastily to meet an emergency breeds diseases which only afflict the grandchildren of those who make them. The rich can secure themselves against the physical but not the moral consequences, and if they can leave their children the gold of the earth they are indifferent to the fact that they are filching from them the gold of the heart, which is the deepest and most subtle offence by which human beings can sin against humanity. The offence, like that of Claudius, is rank and smells to Heaven, and it is upon this that, if we are to restore the architecture of society, we must concentrate. It is a small thing that the few are rich and the many are poor compared with the fact that all are poor in spirit, so poor, indeed, that a tragedy like the war, an heroic convulsion like the Russian Revolution, can leave us unmoved, numbed by the silence in which we live because our fathers have left us an inheritance of much earthly gold and have robbed us of that which should shine in our hearts. They have built us a city of Finance when we looked for a city of God, and we are ashamed because that which is handed on to us with so much pride arouses in us no joy, not even a fleeting pleasure; a dull magnificence, a massive ugliness, cannot compensate for the lack of form, colour and character which we, in our eagerness, desire. The fundamental fact in the present crisis in the evolution of humanity is the inability of the young to accept the society which their elders have so industriously, and with such an appalling sacrifice of life, shaped for them. It is not that they will not, but that they cannot, accept it. Its form does not correspond to their needs or their desires. Its conveniencies, its luxuries can be accepted, but to no particular purpose. It is not enough to go on digging out material and energy from this extraordinary planet. The force of the earth may be tremendous, but

Man is its most miraculous instrument, its most supple and varied; and society to be tolerable must be not only a means to daily bread, but also an expression as supple and varied as Man himself. Otherwise it becomes so oppressive that it must be destroyed. No one wants to destroy it, but every one who is mentally alive wants to overhaul and reshape it and to remove from it all vestiges of tyranny. Dullness and ugliness are created by tyranny, and we find ourselves suffering not from the tyranny of persons but from the tyranny of systems by which men who sacrifice understanding for power are so placed that their words and deeds can influence the lives of millions of their fellows.

It may be said that the stupidity of men is such that they deserve any system that they can be induced to create, but the objection to the present system is precisely that it is not *created,* but rather manufactured piecemeal, to meet the need of each day as it arises, and being so manufactured it denies the creative impulse which is the source of human happiness. There is in the stupidest man the element of devotion. Alone he has not the courage of it. With others it can stir in him and give him that joy without which he cannot live. This is perfectly well known to those who profit by the existing system, and they have attained an abominable skill in confusing this element of devotion in simple men with prejudice and inflamed passion. Those who profit by the simplicity of human beings will not admit how simple they are, and treat them as though they were as cunning and as ruthless as themselves. In situation after situation when the uttered truth could resolve the central difficulties a lie is told to create confusion in which those things that cannot be done openly are accomplished in secret. Those who, having power, are trustees for the people do not trust the people. It is true that complicated economic problems cannot be decided by the mass intelligence, but the greater problems of right or wrong can be, and in the long run always are so decided. The trouble is, that under existing conditions the run is so devilish long that moral decisions are always made years, perhaps generations, after the event, when other problems have arisen, in turn to be shelved in favour of more superficial aspects of the conditions that give rise to them. For instance, when British workers, finding they cannot marry for lack of houses, say so, they are asked to consider the question of the exportation of aliens. Just as material problems are settled by continual expansion (Imperialism), so moral problems are dealt with by a continual shuffling and hedging. The fault lies in the mentality brought to bear on these matters, and the mentality is defective because the spirit is impoverished, and the spirit is impoverished by the attempt to deal with humanity and its erratic career only on the basis of calculable things, leaving out everything that is incalculable though discernible, not, moving through an individual at all powerful, but, moving through the mass, irresistible.

It is because there is such a movement in the mass that youth, aware of it, cannot accept the society in which the aged take their pride. Great towns, railways, aeroplanes, airships, liners, warships, submarines, are all very well in their way, but the young men ask, do they or do they not intensify the adventure of life, or do they merely enslave millions for no particular purpose save to give a few men the apparent but fundamentally false pleasure of efficiency in organising work on the grand scale without ascertaining what the effects of such organisation are, except those which are recorded in a banker's ledger? When young men look away from the ledger they see Manchester, Pittsburg, Johannesburg, Newcastle, Essen, Lille, South Wales, Glasgow—the squalor and misery with which they are filled, and the figures that so dazzle their elders have no gleam for them. They are, rather, meaningless and detestable, for they are only ciphers. Much is made, nothing is created. Society enables men to exist—which they could do without it—and it inhibits their will to live. So powerful has organisation been to procure this unhappy result that definition becomes an almost hopelessly difficult task, because words, like institutions, have been robbed of their meaning. To use words in their full sense is to create misunderstanding, for they are only addressed to a faint echo of what they once signified. Words, like men, are ghosts of themselves, and not even ferro-concrete has succeeded in making human society solid. Almost it would seem that the more existence is heaped up with material wealth, the more fantastic and ephemeral it becomes. That is because it yields less to the spirit in whose light, beaconing from generation to generation, is the only permanence, the only continuity, that is vouchsafed to us. Kindle the spirit and even the deadening organisations that tick out figures in ledgers must be turned to the purpose of enlarging and vivifying consciousness of that permanence and that continuity. Kindle the spirit and we have a lamp wherewith to explore the darkness in which we are suffered to exist. We may then see things as they really are, and we may, seeing even one thing clearly, be shocked and delighted into perception of the intimate relationship of all things: for the truth shines everywhere, being the light by which men and the universe have their transient existence. Without that vision we are driven into the futility either of argument or of dogma, and definition will escape us.

II

HUMANITY

II

HUMANITY

WHATEVER happens men and women must eat, drink and breed like other animals. Their other activities depend upon whether they perform these functions well or ill. That is so obvious as to be hardly worth stating, were it not that it is so obvious as most often to escape the notice of eminent persons, bent, as eating, drinking and breeding are made easy and pleasurable for them, upon preserving their eminence. High ideals are a luxury as unintelligible as caviare or champagne to the man or woman who has to meet a three-pound expenditure on Saturday with twenty-nine shillings. Even when the newspapers ask him or her to think in millions (in other words, to think Imperially), the difference between five shillings and half-a-crown remains. That is one great cause of the disastrous split in humanity. Domestic economy is inexorable, whereas in the economy of Finance the difference between five shillings and half-a-crown disappears. Persons above a certain standard in the scale of income adopt the outlook of Finance, leaving the rest to drudge along with the dreary outlook dictated by the domestic budget. The breach, then, is not so much between poverty and wealth—that might be bridged—as between care and carelessness, two states of mind which cannot find a common language, and therefore use the same ideas and words in different senses. That this has always been the case is no reason why it should always be so, and, indeed, organisation and education have made it impossible for it to continue. The present tendency is to induce everybody to forget the difference between five shillings and half-a-crown, but that difference remains and will have to be faced. There comes a point at which old creditors cannot be met by making new ones. Humanity has to face its creditors. That is the dramatic moment at which we have arrived at the beginning of the twentieth century. Men have tried to avoid it by killing each other, but the fact remains that we have spent our moral capital before it was realised, and are too heavily in debt to the human intellect and the human spirit. If it were only a matter of digging more wealth out of the earth we could set to and dig cheerfully enough, but we have been made aware that the earth is a very small part of the universe, and that the universe is governed by certain principles which appear in human affairs as moral. Roughly, it may be said that every advantage won by humanity over the other elements of creation has to be paid for by work. Now, drudgery is not work. It is a base currency, and we have for too long paid for our advantages in drudgery shuffled over on to the shoulders of the poor and the helpless.

As an example of work let us take, as an extreme instance, the case of a man and a woman who are what is called in love. Nature supplies them in the first instance with tremendous energy, electric and vivifying, for her own purposes of reproduction. That energy will carry them to a certain point of union, but no farther. Nature's energy ebbs; its freshness is dulled by habit, and without effort—that is, work, on the part of the lovers—that energy cannot be humanised in a really fruitful relationship, because elements of mind, character and sympathy must be introduced for which Nature cares not a dew-drop. To other animals the ebbing of Nature's energy is a matter of no importance, but to human beings, who survive by the aid of combination, it is tragically essential that they should defend themselves against it, anticipate it, and raise their relationship from the natural to the human level. In no other way can what is most precious to them—love—continue to exist. That is the supreme human advantage, and, like all the rest, it has to be paid for by work. If it is not paid for, then Nature destroys it exactly as she destroys civilisations that cannot meet their creditors.

This struggle exists in every human activity. It is the prime condition of the existence of humanity, and because it is not admitted such order as we achieve is continually being reduced to chaos. Work avoided, in however small a degree, means drudgery somewhere for some one.

Now, the development and the abuse of machinery have given rise to a general organised conspiracy to avoid work. That conspiracy we call European civilisation, and to preserve it millions of men have been condemned to four years' drudgery in the trenches. No loud-sounding words can make that right.

No one expects a perfect world in which drudgery shall everywhere have been replaced by work. The process of elevation there is as slow as any other stage of evolution, but every man and woman has the right to expect a world in which such disastrous collapses into drudgery shall be avoided. Every man and woman expects it and must work for it. As to the means by which that can be made possible, we shall discover them as we pursue our examination.

Accept, first of all, that work is right and that drudgery is wrong. The reward of work is leisure: the consequence of drudgery is sloth. The proof of the pudding is in the eating, and work and drudgery can be defined by their results. A human being who is really working gains energy by it, up to a point defined by his natural limitations; he gains eagerness, pride in his skill, a fine perception of the nature of his doing. A human being who is engaged in drudgery loses perception, keenness, and is stultified until he becomes the mechanical creature of habit. All human activity can be either work or drudgery, and until that is understood there can be no understanding of humanity whose condition depends upon the degree to which the world's drudgery is dominated by the world's work. At present it is obvious that the world is dominated by human drudgery, which, except in a very few men, has destroyed the capacity for work. The real problem, then, is how to increase that capacity, for it is the lack of it that engenders the appalling waste from which humanity has too long suffered. Human life depends upon human energy, for which that extracted from the earth is not an efficient substitute, though it is a necessary complement, just as tools are the necessary complement of hands. Machines are tools driven by the energy extracted from the earth, but as they are too expensive to be owned and maintained by individuals they are, as a rule, maintained and owned collectively, and the labour necessary to run them is hired as cheaply as possible. Hence has arisen tyranny through the ownership of machines which has replaced tyranny through the ownership of the land. It was a sound but misguided instinct that made the operatives of the early nineteenth century resist every new installation of machinery, because they knew that ownership of machinery, added to ownership of land, meant an intolerable increase to their burden. And so it has proved. The production of wealth has been so enormous that the material status of the physical worker has been improved, but his moral status has been degraded to such an extent that he cannot be passionate even in revolt. If we compare the spirit of the French Revolution with that of the Russian we cannot but be struck with a weakening of fibre, of the degree of force expressed in the later convulsion, and it seems likely that the old order was really destroyed by the first assault, but that those who knew how to profit by that order succeeded in maintaining the semblance of it, even while the new order slowly took shape, as it has been doing ever since in France. Voltaire, Diderot and Rousseau gave expression to the new spirit, or, not to fight shy of the inevitable word, the new religion. Humanity follows very slowly in the wake of its leaders of thought, who are never in a hurry, knowing perfectly well that great changes only come when the increase in the population of the world makes existing economic and political systems embarrassing and uncomfortable. The men of action unfortunately are generally in a hurry and anxious to produce results for which they can be rewarded. They produce such results, but they are nearly always disastrous, preventing and stultifying the ideas which should guide humanity through its crises, and even deriding the thinkers and visionaries whose will they are forced to carry out.

Humanity has a will backed by the creative will which animates the universe. When the will of humanity is thwarted over long stretches of time by the setting up of false authorities there are violent reactions and readjustments, and false authorities are swept away. These violent reactions and readjustments are a waste of energy which in time will have to be obviated in order to meet both the economic necessities of the world and that other moral bill which is now due. The will of humanity, like that of a tree or a flower or a human being, is creative and destroys only to create. When it is unhealthy and exasperated it destroys only for the sake of destruction, and that neither materially nor spiritually can provide any lasting satisfaction, though there is something to be said for an outburst of temper as clearing the air; but it is precisely to control the temper of humanity that authority is needed, for sudden reversions to a primitive and childish state of mind can do an amount of damage which it takes a generation to restore, and a generation requires to do more with its energy than repairing the mischief done by its predecessors.

As the prime condition of human existence is work, so the authority governing that existence emanates from work, and that authority is living or sterile, according as work is kept current or is impeded, continually ennobled or degraded to drudgery. Those who maintain great state or power or mere wealth do so by obtaining doles from the work of millions. As a rule they obtain these doles so indirectly that they regard them as coming from some mysterious source as a reward for their extraordinary merits, or, in many cases, they do not think about it at all, but accept their fortune as in the natural order of things. Kings and priests consider their ease and magnificence as given to them by God, while financiers and manufacturers, who have succeeded those functionaries in the modern organisation of society, accept their enormous incomes as evidence of their capacity for "getting things done," and as proof that the things done needed doing. The structure of society remains the same: doles from the work of millions are gathered together into a source of power which is directed by persons not so much appointed as agreed to, because of their success in attaining a certain position, to maintain which they use the power at their disposal to create more power. Blind to the fact that this power emanates from work, they seek to fortify it with force and divert it from constructive to destructive purposes. Kings and priests had some excuse for such a mistake because they believed themselves to be appointed by God, and that any one who questioned their operations was committing a kind of blasphemy. But financiers and manufacturers have no such excuse, though it may be said for them that they have inherited powers which they have had neither the training nor the opportunity to understand. Henry V could awaken a thrill of loyalty with the cry, "God for Harry, England and St. George!" But a modern soapboiler or newspaper proprietor, who has probably more power than King Henry ever dreamed, can arouse no such enthusiasm, and without enthusiasm the greatest power must dwindle. You may pile up gold, foodstuffs, housing material, all the good and comfortable things of the earth for generations, but there comes a point at which human nature can endure no more, and will sacrifice everything for a thrill, a breath freely drawn, a generous gesture. In such a moment the mightiest power will be shaken to its foundations and the eternal question is asked once more: "By what authority?"

When that question is asked it has been the practice of governors to set one section of humanity against another. Divide and rule. In old times all men were as simple as the ex-Emperor Wilhelm II, and believed that when they fought they fought for God and that God fought with them. Now and henceforth that superstition has lost its validity. Human pugnacity is without its old sanction, and if there are to be wars in future they will be a matter of frank greed, blood-lust and craving for excitement, of which a large proportion of humanity will be ashamed: and not only of war, but of preparations for war. They will ask why the doles extracted from the work of humanity should be put to such a wasteful use, and when they are told that it is to maintain right against wrong they will ask in season and out for definition as the only safeguard against the easily roused passions of the crowd.

Humanity is not, or ought not to be, a crowd, and no section of it should be treated as such, but as a collection of human beings entitled to enjoy the fruits of the earth and of their labour upon it, and the leisure in which to discover in each other those joys without which human life is vastly inferior to that of the beasts, or the bees and ants, or the trees and flowers. Human life is a matter of personal relations. These are the vital necessity, and if they are degraded for the sake of any other element that element is wrong, whatever may be the apparent advantages due to it. Any organisation which degrades those who participate in it is too injurious to be admissible, and human society, at present and for a long time to come, looks like being dependent upon such organisation, creating power without authority for the few, work without leisure for the many. Now, power without authority can only be maintained by trickery and cunning, which, as the dodges are revealed—and they are few and time-honoured—become more barefaced.

European civilisation is at present dominant in the affairs of humanity, and its power over other civilisations increases. It has lost its old sanctions and its old spirit: humanism is dead, Christianity is threadbare: this civilisation persists by its rapacity and its mechanical power. Its engines, constructive and destructive, blast their way through the other civilisations in the quest of the precious raw materials necessary for the maintenance of urban existence. Everywhere they destroy and do not replace old habits, old religions, ancient forms of society; and they offer nothing in return except a crude arrangement by which the doles extracted from the work of human beings can rapidly be accumulated into a power directed solely to the production of more wealth from the earth. It may be said that these methods do, on the whole, increase the well-being of the disorganised multitudes who were formerly scratching a meagre living from inhospitable tracts of the world, but it is incontestable that the violence with which millions of men and women have been uprooted from their traditional existence has produced a blight which is probably the greatest affliction from which humanity has ever suffered. It has forced upon men and women everywhere a consciousness for which they have no equipment, so that they live in an increasing pain and are isolated as they never were from each other. The result bears a superficial resemblance to decadence, but it is rather a paralysis of stagnation, almost a fear of the new mode of living that has become necessary, combined with a fatalistic fore-knowledge that European civilisation, in attempting to conquer humanity, will be absorbed by it.

What is happening is this: European civilisation is attempting to conquer the earth for the benefit of the Europeans, or rather of the comparative few who possess economic power, and is doing so without the slightest regard for humanity. The better to achieve this purpose it was necessary to dispose of the insurgent elements in the European populations, who were accordingly turned against each other in the war of 1914-18, which effectively disposed of the chances of a proletarian internationalism intruding upon the internationalism of the economically powerful, bent on establishing control of raw materials. The war, then, has been only an element in the long struggle between those whose aim is to control raw materials, and those whose aim is to control labour. In this struggle humanity is not considered at all, because each side is consumed with dread of the other. It is not a conflict between autocracy and democracy in the old political sense, for politics are very remote from facts. The conflict is between autocracy and democacy in the industrial sense, and the battle is in the industrial field. Until it is fought out there will not be much room for the normal healthy activities which make the sum of human happiness, and the race will live an uneasy, distracted and dissatisfied existence. Raw materials are necessary, labour is necessary. Out of these two have grown two conflicting interests whose wrangling day by day destroys human hopes and increases that despair to which the greater part of the men and women of the century have been reduced. It is an old quarrel arising from the denial of the right of him who works to have a voice in the direction of the dole which is taken from his work for social purposes, and until that right is established the quarrel cannot be resolved. To this must be added the denial of social purposes as meaning the purposes of humanity, though that has grown out of, rather than contributed to, the quarrel, the two parties to which are blinded by the diversion of their energies from their work to their feud.

As the struggle grows in intensity old conceptions are destroyed, indolence becomes more and more impossible, and we are slowly forced to take a simple view both of ourselves and of our situation. Millions have died and are dying of violence or neglect, and such death has its inevitable reaction upon life—poisonous, stultifying, enervating; and that burden, unlike the material load, cannot be passed on to the poor. Increased production is not a sufficient antidote to a moral infection, for under the present social system it would simply mean a vaster accumulation of the doles taken from work done to be spent on the purchase of raw materials. It is not enough to cry out against an exploiting class: humanity is exploiting humanity, and until the social system is amended cannot help doing so.

The evil has grown out of the fear of poverty: not merely of the discomfort, but even more of the inertia that poverty brings. If a man must endure squalor, dirt, vermin, lack of privacy, and gnawing anxiety from week to week, he cannot but lose his self-respect, and with that gone, there is no hope of his achieving pride of work without which his existence is savourless. His manhood is dissipated and he becomes the drudge of his family, of his own enfeebled appetites, of those who employ him for as little as he can be got to accept. Small wonder, then, that from this horror men struggle to escape, but they do not escape if their efforts are directed to thrusting others down into it. For men are more than brothers: they are all parts of one soul, and the suffering of any portion of it affects the whole.

The survival of the fittest was a phrase applied to species: humanity as a whole may take pride in its survival, but every part of humanity owes its existence to the evolutionary effort of the whole. A huge effort is now becoming discernible, an attempt to achieve more consciousness, and the war and the class-war, considered in this relation, take shape as perverse endeavours to resist that effort. Men are reluctant to change their minds, and when, their ideas falling behind the necessity of the time, they suffer they are apt to attribute their suffering to those whom they have learned to regard as their enemies. When a man stumbles over a brick and hurts his toe he will often seek relief in kicking the brick. Men have no enemies other than themselves: they are assured in their mastery of Nature. It is only in self-mastery that they are uneasy and uncomfortably aware of futility. Self-mastery is only to be won through work: drudgery destroys it, and drudgery can only be destroyed by the removal of poverty, dread of which is the prime motive force in the present organisation of society.

Can it be done? It can and it must be done if, as I maintain, humanity is engaged in a tremendous evolutionary effort. This new consciousness, eager to explore the world revealed by mechanical power, most eager to discover the buried treasure of the human heart, will not tolerate the drag upon its activity of a dread akin to that which has been so patiently conquered, namely, the fear of Nature. The only remaining question is as to whether this conquest shall be achieved through disaster or through triumph, through a collapse upon force or through the assertion of mind and will. It is a lamentable fact that hitherto great social changes have only been brought about through hunger, but now it seems to be within the bounds of possibility that the hunger of the spirit may prove to be a swifter and more effective explosive force than the hunger of the belly. Certainly the hunger of the spirit is the force with which we have to reckon—old illusions, old fables have lost their efficacy to satisfy men and women gathered in such huge masses as they are to-day. Even the lies with which their minds are fed are but perversions of the truth: they have not the charm and the potency of religious and poetical inventions. Gods and kings are in exile: men and women know that their rulers are men and women like themselves, and they are in a mood to force them to acknowledge their responsibility, not to any imagined power or majesty, but to the immediate and real authority of humanity. That is the issue, and nothing can confuse it. Through history it has become more and more urgent, but until the earth was explored and conquered it could be obscured by a thousand and one minor quarrels. Now issue is joined, and there can be no rest until the principle is established that the doles taken from the daily toil of humanity shall be used for humanity to lighten its physical toil that it may be free for spiritual effort. That is the aim of all human endeavour. It can now be clearly seen, and there should be an end of all attempts to disguise it with smaller aims or to perpetuate the diversion to material ends of forces whose purposes are spiritual. The desire of every living thing is to discover the Newfoundland of its own soul. In human beings that desire is conscious, and in them their natural functions are but the means to that end. They have agreed to society in order as little as possible to be impeded by those functions, and perpetually they urge onwards to enrich society with their discovery. Exploration of the earth is but the symbol of that other voyage which is life, and the mystics sunk in contemplation enrich humanity no less than those who reveal far countries and bring back charted the imagined oceans. Humanity, urged on by this quest of the soul, has incidentally discovered the boundless wealth of this planet, but only incidentally. The powers revealed have been so immense as to dazzle and overwhelm the mind so that the art to use those powers has been neglected. Men are, for the lack of such art, simply rich or poor: living one kind of life or another, and in both character is of less immediate value than cunning, because in the fever engendered by lack of organisation material values obscure spiritual, and property dominates life. The suffering so created is barren, and prevents the operation of the fruitful suffering which is the creative element in human life without which joy cannot be released. The joy of humanity is captive, for a space, but joy is indestructible and will be free. Those who would confine it do but postpone the destruction which must come upon them and upon human society. Joy in its freedom destroys that it may create, destroys the old and the outworn, cleanses and purges and gives in abundance: while greed destroys only that it may take, and heaps up dead things that make life take on the semblance of a tomb, the nature of which no magnificence can disguise.

Before humanity lies the most momentous choice of its destiny. It is a choice that has to be made in millions of instances every day, and the inadequate structure of society forces upon the vast majority the wrong choice. With almost every breath we draw we have to choose between life and death, and almost always, so constrained are we by false appearances and promises of ease for the moment, we choose death. Failure to seize and to employ one opportunity means a proportionate weakness in facing the next. As with the individual, so with the mass. The grand opportunity will be upon us in the next generation. Europe has to accept or to deny its responsibility to humanity, to choose between life and death. It is to help, in however small a degree, in seeing that the choice is truly made, and that the human mind shall seek out the human will, its only trustworthy power, that these words are written.

III

THE SOCIAL CONTRACT

III

THE SOCIAL CONTRACT

ROUSSEAU believed that there was a Golden Age and that Man was as beneficent as Nature. We know that Nature is not altogether beneficent: she is equally maleficent. And so is Man: both creative and destructive, both good and evil, and as dependent upon the dual principle as he is upon light and darkness. An excess of goodness is as enervating to human life as a monotony of sunlight. Humanity is as varied as the sea, and its desire is pitched beyond good and evil, between which there is an ever-widening swing of the pendulum, necessitating a continual emendation of the social conceptions of good and evil. As this change is continuous the stability of society depends ultimately upon man's loyalty to humanity, which must operate through a number of intermediate loyalties, and it is precisely here that conflict is continually arising. A man's loyalty to his fellow-men, his contemporaries, is not the same as his loyalty to humanity. When conflict arises the less should be sacrificed to the greater, whereas most commonly in practice it is demanded that the greater should be sacrificed to the less, because a man's life is too easily bounded by what appear to be his immediate interests, or, if he can see beyond them, he is too often forced by pressure into limiting his vision to the apparent advantages of his social group, his family, trade, or nation, especially at times when it seems that these advantages are threatened by those of another group. He is then reminded of his obligations and is expected to be guided by the voice of the majority, who in their passion would usurp his loyalty, relying upon some such idea as the social contract expounded by Rousseau at a time when society was emerging from feudalism. We have travelled far since then, and have become scientific in our habit of mind, and need some definition of our various loyalties.

Every man carries beneath his hat his innumerable ancestors, and is their representative in the assembly of humanity. His immediate loyalty is to them; that is, to himself, and by observing that loyalty he best observes his loyalty to humanity, and if the intermediate loyalties rouse conflict, he, as the trustee of his ancestors to humanity, must abide by his trust and range himself against the loyalty which by raising conflict has proved itself to be superfluous and unnecessary. A loyalty which demands action without vision is contrary to humanity, for humanity is governed by vision and by nothing else. Without it chaos and anarchy prevail, as at intervals of two or three generations they invariably do. Human beings must be fed, but the lesser purposes of humanity are best served by devotion to the greater, just as the will of a section of humanity is most easily and effectively achieved when it is consonant with the will of humanity, which rests not, but drives on unceasingly towards its goal. The most discernible purpose of that will is not to rest content with the apparent limitations of existence, whereas it becomes the aim of certain individuals and sections of humanity to turn institutions into limitations added to those set by natural law. To the free spirit of man, or the spirit that desires freedom, that is intolerable, for, to that spirit, all things human, both good and evil, should tend to increase man's knowledge of and love for humanity, for only through these can the unattainable absolute be approached. Hence, the perpetual revolt of man not so much against his institutions as against the uses to which they are put. Institutions do not greatly change: the organisations of public and private life depend upon a few devices which the more they change the more they are the same. Every man is both himself and a social being, and the only power that can reconcile these two entities is his own conscience. The social contract is signed in a man's own soul or not at all, and if it be not signed he remains a turbulent and anarchic creature parasitic upon humanity, and continually sacrificing life to the satisfaction of his own appetites. He remains the prey of every trick and fraud designed to cheat him of his birthright. Kingcraft, priestcraft, mobcraft have him at their mercy, and can force him at any moment to sacrifice the loyalties imposed upon him in his birth to the advantages of his group. This has been the order of society for so long that it is accepted as in the nature of things, though with the slow enlargement of groups perception has been widened, greater freedom has been won; and though the pressure from the majority has increased, it has served to heighten the courage of the minority, who have become aware of the true nature of the social contract, and who know that whenever the interest of a section of humanity is exalted above humanity's laws that contract is violated.

As every individual is, by that contract, a trustee, so every institution is vested with its powers in trust and not absolutely. The trend of social evolution is away from law towards equity, and from property to the principle of trust. This may tend to limit the opportunities for material adventure, but it releases energy for the adventures of the soul. It spreads responsibility and liability more evenly, and makes it more possible for more men and women to realise the social contract to which they owe their existence, and its relief from drudgery, the increasing value of their work and their growing pride in it. This process continually breaks down barriers, first the family, then the caste, then the kingdom, then the nation, as more and more co-operation is needed. Those who resist this process for the sake of a long row of ciphers in a banker's ledger may get the ciphers, but they obtain nothing else.

For them, even those human beings through whom they should live become ciphers, and they might be left to their miserable fate, but that they are in a position to force their cipher-vision upon the multitudes who by dread of poverty are forced to work for them.

Than this cipher-vision no more powerful means was ever invented for obscuring the social contract. The devices of organised religion were trivial compared with it; the mirage of military glory with which kings maintained their state is by comparison impotent. It transfers life from the good earth to paper, and its problems are worked out there. Those problems that defy such solution are ignored, and to prevent their arising economic power is ruthlessly used to reduce the workers of the world to slavery.

Never was humanity in a more tragic plight than now, when its marvellous ingenuity and heroic power are employed for the creation of ciphers and nothing else. To that the grandeur that was Greece and the glory that was Rome have been reduced. Such thinking as can force its way through this nullity is done in a vacuum, and can achieve nothing to disturb these complacent 0's. Except by the shifting of ciphers from one ledger to another, or from page to page of the same ledger, nothing can be done, and yet the control of the ciphers remains in the hands of men who have sacrificed all knowledge of the social contract to collect them. Power remains with them in every section of society, and in every section when alarm at the approach of disaster becomes articulate the inhabitants of it are urged to defend themselves against an external enemy. Men are badged and numbered and given allotted tasks in that defence to which their normal humane occupations are sacrificed, and *public* powers are used to augment *private* profits.

That is the fatal flaw in the present organisation of society. In old times, kings and priests used their public powers in their philosophy, if not always in their practice, to the public advantage. They, like the humblest peasant, commended their souls to God, but the modern rulers of the world have no faith except in ciphers, and they are, in such philosophy as they possess, divorced from the life of the people. A great merchant can pretend that the expansion of his fortune is proof of his service to society, but there is no check on his use of it, and nothing to show that the service he has rendered might not have been better done by other methods and by a proper and conscientious use of public powers. Yet the mischief between the rich and the poor is that, while the rich are dealing in ciphers the poor have to grapple with the hard actualities of existence. Thus they speak different languages, use the same words often in contrary senses: the poor attaching a concrete meaning to everything, the rich thinking in the abstractions of commercialism. Those who lend their money upon interest to industrial undertakings have as a rule not the slightest knowledge of their working, and therefore accept the apparent prosperity shown in annual reports with entire complacency, and, of course, without a thought of its bearing upon the social contract. As this polite usury is the basis of modern civilisation it is here that we find the source of its inhumanity. The great men of finance recognise their responsibility to their shareholders, but not their responsibility to their managers and workpeople, who, in the interest of the shareholders, are paid as little as they can be got to accept. Certainly we have advanced very far from the hideous abuses of the early nineteenth century, but we have not yet succeeded in establishing justice as a principle in commercial organisations from which necessarily has grown the structure of society. For lack of justice there is no liberty in that structure, and for lack of liberty there is no health, and the social contract cannot operate because it is thwarted by the lop-sided contracts which it is the aim of every business man to secure.

Authority in any community is developed out of the contract agreed between the individual as private and as public person, which is forced upon him first of all in family life, later at school, and finally as a citizen. Directly a man admits, as he must, the rights of others to his services in return for theirs, he enters upon a contract—immediately with the persons surrounding him, but ultimately with humanity—and authority, liberty and justice depend upon the due observance of that contract. In Europe, suffering under a fever of nationalism, it has been assumed that the contract is between the individual and the nation to which he belongs. There is such a contract, but it is only a clause in the greater, and should be a means to its fulfilment. That it has not been so is due to the economic injustice of the social system, by which men have been forced to sacrifice the greater to the less, and in foregoing their own egoism to contribute to that of their nation.

There is no need here to labour the tragic consequences which have brought us suddenly face to face with the need for authority and for tracing it to its source. It lies in the social contract by which the individual acknowledges his social relationship in return for the advantages that can be won for humanity. To preserve that social contract amid the innumerable other contracts that have to be entered into Government is agreed upon and appointed as trustee; and hitherto the trust has been betrayed in favour of the rich and against the poor, because there has been no visible authority beyond Government in the various communities, and no means by which public opinion all the world over can make itself felt; and yet from every breach of trust on the part of the various manipulated Governments humanity has suffered disastrously. It was this long tale of suffering that caused Nietzsche to cry out for a race of supermen, and Kropotkin and Bakunin, coming with freshness of energy to a worn civilisation, to acclaim Anarchy as the solution of its problems. Meanwhile, before these prophets could be understood, there has come a crisis which by sheer economic necessity enforces simplification and an attempted understanding. On the one hand, the trusts and cartels, on the other, the Trades Unions tighten up their machinery dreading lest the rest of the world should sink into the famine and bloodshed which, for lack of machinery, social and industrial, has been the fate of Russia. However, as the crisis came from this tightening of machinery by both capital and labour, it seems improbable that further efforts in that direction will find a solution.

Taking Great Britain as a typical industrial community of this unfortunate age, we find that the public is alternately held up by the operations of the trusts restricting imports and the strikes of the Trades Unions against those operations. The accounts of this continual conflict given in the newspapers are misleading and prejudiced, and it is nowhere suggested that these two vast machines should be conscientiously used for humanity instead of against each other. Both sides cry politically "Great Britain for the British," oblivious of the fact that Great Britain is only important as an enlightened member of humanity, and as trustee of a great part of the earth's products. The contract between Great Britain and the individual is insisted upon: that between Great Britain and humanity is denied. The trust principle is ignored and the individual British make their social contracts only to have them thwarted by the action of their Government. The result is serious not only for the British but for humanity, for it means that the British Empire sprawls between the mechanised energy of America and the spiritual energy of Russia, and prevents the formation of the society which both those energies desire. Both America and Russia look to Great Britain for guidance and help, and receive nothing but the cry of a wounded egoism. Great Britain to the rest of humanity has been something more than an island: she has meant certain liberal and humane principles by which the idealism of more fiery races can be made practicable. But now it seems that with that practical sense, which so frequently tyrannises over her nobility, she is bent on making her Victory as dreary and horrible as her Sunday, so that her citizens will be only too glad to return to work under any conditions. . . . That would be all very well if a new world were not in the making, in which the new consciousness that is beginning to dawn in the east must play its part. That consciousness has given a new direction to the human will: a direction not dreamed of by Adam Smith or Cobden or even John Bright. It is profoundly and unalterably aware of the social contract and is insisting upon it as the essential element in government; and because the social contract disturbs the contracts to which the financiers owe their power, they are resisting them with every available means. The admission of the social contract, as a natural bargain between the individual and humanity, implies the revision of those contracts. It leads to what Nietzsche attempted, the transvaluation of all values, and to a drastic alteration not only of the structure but of the basis of society. It means that society also, as well as individual men, approaches God through humanity, and that men will no longer look for authority from on high, but within themselves and their personal relationships. Once admitted, it can be recognised and acknowledged wherever it shows itself, but authority and the social contract upon which it depends can only be seen through love, the active and passionate love preached by Jesus Christ, but, alas! perverted into a milky resignation, which perhaps has more than anything else contributed to the triumph of injustice, now at last so intolerable that men must admit the spiritual means by which they live and rediscover love. Without that the tyranny of machinery must continue, and human traffic will be impeded to the lasting hurt of civilisation. In the chaos of the last century we invented policemen to regulate the traffic; now we have to invent some means of regulating the policemen. In other words, we have to insist that the social contract which binds individuals shall also bind the governments elected by them, and that just as individuals have abandoned duelling in favour of Law, so Governments shall abandon war. Just as the wearing of swords was found to impede the operation of the social contract, so it has been with national armaments. The social contract is there, just as the principle of marriage is there, as an inherent condition in the existence of humanity. We have nothing else. If it is denied we are driven back upon force which settles nothing except that the innocent suffer for the guilty, and, what we already know too well, that the fathers have eaten sour grapes and the children's teeth are set on edge.

IV

PATRIARCHALISM

IV

PATRIARCHALISM

THE most vigorous and persistent race in Europe is the Jewish, which has forced its God and its domestic institutions upon the subtler and more distracted peoples. There is no Jewish Empire—unless the world, through the Rothschilds, the Sassoons, the Cassels, the Speyers, be regarded as such—and no Jewish hegemony. Rather do the Jews desire that which they cannot achieve, absorption into the other races and a share in that beauty which those races pursue. The Jews are weary, it seems, of the curse upon Ahasuerus. They buy the treasures of Greece and Rome, but they cannot buy the civilising principle. Nowhere can they take root, nowhere can they draw sustenance from humanity as other races do who build and destroy and build again. The Jew clings to his God and his family, and dares not look beyond them. He amasses riches to the glory of his God and the splendour of his family, but remains a captive in Babylon. He cannot desert the patriarchal principle. His world is a pyramid built up to Jehovah, and the father or patriarch, as the nearest to Jehovah, is invested with authority. It may be that the Jews, having a strong social sense, cling to this arrangement, none other being yet forthcoming, and it may be that to it they owe the advantages they enjoy in the greedy scramble which is accepted as life in Europe; but it is certain that they also owe to it their unalterable squalor and their hunger for beauty. With a mournful envy they regard the adventurousness of other races, but their traditions are too strong for them, and they remain—Jews, when their desire is to be Europeans. A pathetic desire this, for there are as yet no Europeans, no European tradition, only a turbulent and rather hectic attempt to assert that there is one. The Jew in his financial outlook is European, but in other matters he accepts outwardly the tradition of the community to which he is attached, while inwardly he remains solemnly faithful to Jehovah—truly religious, because religion is his life, justifying even such plunder as he indulges in as being done at the expense of the irreligious.

Religion consists in a man's belief, not in what he believes. The Jew believes in his family and his God, and therefore has a direct aim set for his activities. In what does the modern European believe? Goethe, Wagner, Beethoven have urged him to believe in Europe, but their insistence has been in vain. The Jews have given Europe a certain financial structure, but there their contribution ends, because the Europeans cannot yet be European. Unlike the Jews, they are in the mass unaware of and insensible to the beauty that Europe has created. Wars of religion, giving place to wars of patriotism, have robbed them of their capacity for brotherhood, so that even socialism is in the different countries tainted with nationalism. The wars of Europe have given the Jews the opportunity, which they have not been slow to use, of building up the financial structure which has enabled the Europeans, in spite of their distractions, to dominate the earth; but that domination stops short at finance, because the Jews have nothing else to contribute, their God and their conception of the family being rejected in favour of a wider individualism, and the principle of spiritual equality growing in acceptance with the gradual emancipation of women. The result is, that while the Jews are in a position to dominate Europe, they have not the mentality necessary, and can only manipulate Europe's and the world's finances. That is an essential, but at the same time a subordinate, element in government, and it is forced into undue predominance by this unfortunate *impasse*. Jewish finance—and in all its operations it reveals its origin—pulls in one direction, the evolution of Europe in another. The Jews perhaps more than any other people know the meaning of the social contract, but their interpretation is contrary to the sense in which it is desired by other men. The Jews by their tradition are driven to use their control of finance to establish patriarchalism, while the Europeans desire their society to promote liberty; and the two aims are incompatible. As Europe must live, the inhabitants of the unhappy Continent are constrained to accept a patriarchal financial system, impressing itself on all their activities, which are directed to the abolition of patriarchalism. There can be no doubt which of these two forces will in the long run win, but until the Europeans become European it will be a very long run.

This conflict is very much deeper than that between Capital and Labour, which indeed arises out of it. In Great Britain, like so much else, it is, or has been, covered up, as the British owe a great deal of their ascendancy to their skill in confusing issues, and also to their having assimilated the Jewish financial system as a powerful aid and natural ally of their own patriarchal system of land tenure. The result has been that, during the stress of the war, the slowly built up attempts at democracy have given way and a patriarchal form of government has been established, although the enthusiasm of the people has been for liberty and democracy. Now, patriarchalism can only persist by the imposition of discipline. In old days that was obtained through a religion promising rewards or threatening punishment hereafter; but, science having destroyed the efficacy of religion, discipline can now only be imposed by conscription or enforced obedience to a power that has no authority. The existing form of government depends upon conscription, which will therefore remain until the existing form of government is altered, and that cannot be until the financial system is changed.

Masses of men in revolt rarely know precisely against what they are in rebellion. They are roused partly by their physical discomfort, but more by the gnawing discontent of their own helplessness. The pugnacity of man is in the long run directed against his own shadow.

In the European countries the prevalent anti-Semitism is not altogether directed by Catholic prejudice. It is to a great extent an instinctive revolt against the Jewish financial system, and as that has its centre in London they cannot attain it and are exasperated by their own futility; and the more easily, therefore, is their animosity diverted into the service of nationalism, by which since the French Revolution patriarchal institutions have been able to preserve themselves until, through all the shocks and alarms of war, they have crystallised out into High Finance, whose operations are verily those of a God of Battles, and bear a terrible resemblance to the actions of Jehovah as recorded in the Old Testament. But the funds manipulated by High Finance are composed of the doles extracted from the labours of the workers of the world, who, as education spreads among them, want to know why they should be enslaved by their work. They are enslaved because the power they create is in accordance with ideas which that power has rendered inadequate, ideas which, moreover, have been proved to be false by the world's brain workers. However, as the machinery of government was evolved from those ideas and the machinery remains unaltered, the ideas remain unchanged. No reform is ever effected until the machinery by which an abuse or an anachronism is maintained breaks down, and those reformers who look for a sudden enlightened upheaval as the result of their eloquence are doomed to disappointment. Society is a matter of machinery, and is beneficial or injurious to humanity in accordance with the ideas by which that machinery is controlled. Patriarchal ideas were all very well when they were in accordance with humanity's aspiration for a Heaven beyond the grave, but since humanity's aspiration is for liberty this side death, the ideas governing the machinery of society must be brought into harmony with it. The idea in an old man's head cannot be altered, and this is a matter for youth alive to, and thrilling with, the new consciousness that has come into humanity. The old men cling to High Finance and its patriarchalism, and cannot understand the meaning of the young men and their demand for change. To the old men High Finance has been an end in itself, like all things patriarchal, while the young men demand that it shall be a means to the gradual fulfilment of their aspiration. The old men are astonished: they have toiled and schemed and planned and plotted, and have woven a web from whose embrace the young men are intent upon escaping. The old men say: "You must produce more"; the young men say: "It is useless to produce anything until the tyranny of High Finance is broken." At this point in the argument the old men lose their tempers, because they have been unaware of any tyranny, and they cannot realise that the young men are speaking not only for their generation but also for the soul of humanity. The tragedy through which they have passed has made them prophetic. In them sounds again the prophecy voiced by Walt Whitman after the American tragedy of the last century. They demand that human society shall be based solidly upon the earth, and the right of all men to extract sufficient food from it, and no longer be kept perilously dependent upon a hypothesis, for patriarchalism is no more. It rests entirely upon the ill-founded assumption that a man in power is *ex officio* hallowed with authority from above. If we have learned anything from science, it is that natural forces are more subtle than the human mind can possibly conceive, and that if there be a divine will it operates through the will of all species and all living things. Before this was or could be realised, the human capacity for illusion being what it is, patriarchalism was a sufficiently rough-and-ready means of introducing order into the affairs of communities; but as these grew from hundreds into thousands, and from thousands into millions, the means have lost their efficacy. The power created by enormous populations could no longer be left unchecked in the hands of the obvious persons, and accordingly committees were appointed to control them, though still no means was found to restrain the centralisation of power. Vast empires grew, and with them the control of millions of lives passed into the hands of a few men; but as power increased authority waned, and for the lack of it power passed from the ruling castes to the classes who lent them the money with which to rule, so that government in the modern world has become a matter of usury. There is a class which lends, and a class which works to pay the interest on money lent, and there is a small class of professional money-lenders who take a large commission on all loans, and it is with these that power rests. Now, while the working class deals for the most part in cash transactions, the others live by credit, and, as every one knows from his own experience, credit is a far more supple instrument of currency than cash. The working classes of the world have no credit, and are therefore at the mercy of those classes who have it; and these classes use it patriarchally—that is to say, tyrannically—for the aggrandisement which is a legacy from Jehovah, whose instructions to Abraham have remained the guiding principle in human affairs in spite of all protest from reformers and religious teachers and non-conformist sects. The aggrandisement which the poor have been denied in their own lives they have been suffered to enjoy as members now of a Church, now of a nation, but always they have had to pay very dearly for it, until at last they are in the mood to pay no more.

With this mood the young men of to-day are in entire sympathy, while the old men cannot understand it, throw up their hands, and imagine that the universe is crashing about their ears. What *is* crashing is the system of usury upon which society has too long depended, and with it go the usurers, whose power of granting or withholding credit must in the future be administered with authority, if only—to put it at its lowest—to check the waste, peculation and corruption without which those who cherish patriarchal power cannot maintain it. Even more than upon the waste incurred in armaments does such power depend upon waste in bribery, multiplication of offices, contracting and sub-contracting, political manipulation, and administrative duplication, by which a ruling caste can maintain its inaccessibility to criticism and democratic pressure. As the basis of the ruling caste in modern communities has changed from a birth to a money qualification, and as with that change the old patriarchal sanction has disappeared, parliamentary institutions have become a bulwark between the ruling caste and the proletariat, and, so easy has it become, in the absence of any sanction, to manipulate those institutions, that the extension of the franchise serves but to strengthen the bulwark.

Suppose, for a moment, that, as seems probable, a revolution takes place in Great Britain, as the result of which the joint-stock company system becomes obsolete and industries are nationalised. The ruling caste of shareholders will be replaced by a ruling caste of officials, who will not be easily distinguishable from the persons they have supplanted. A government dominated by Trade Union machinery would not be very different from a government dominated by capitalistic machinery, except in so far as the system of delegation is an advance on representation. There would still remain the patriarchal idea that people must do as they are told to do, and that governments exist for the purpose of giving orders and are inherently disciplinary. Hence the curious theory which prevails in Great Britain that a government cannot say "Yes" or "No" without reference to a commission, which shall, after due deliberation, report; and hence, too, the equally curious necessity for talking one language in the constituencies, another in the House of Commons. The notion is that a government being given power must use it, wisely or unwisely, or appear weak; whereas, in truth, the desire of plain men is that governments shall govern as little as possible. The nationalisation of industries does not mean that they shall be conducted by government departments, but that government departments shall be trustees to see that they are economically administered, with a due regard for what is financially possible and for the best interests of all concerned. The humble workers in industries like mining, the railways, and the docks appeal to government for nationalisation because without a trustee they have found themselves in a hopeless position. The patriarchalism of Private Enterprise could not give them the wealth it promised, and they ask that the system shall be amended.

If a man works hard as a producer and at the end of a week finds that he has not been able to supply his needs as a consumer, he knows perfectly well, without any theory of economics, that there is waste somewhere, and he wants it corrected. As an individual he can do nothing, but in combination with the other workers in his trade, all in the same plight, he can become articulate; and if his grievance remains unheard, he can withhold his labour until it is considered and if possible redressed. At the other end of the scale, if a man did precious little for a year and at the end of that time found himself richer by many thousands of pounds, he would, if he had a living conscience, recognise that he was profiting by economic injustice, and he would associate his strange case with the complaints reaching him from all sides. He would agree that here was a case for the modification of law by equity. He might even, if his conscience was very acute, realise that he was living under a system that made him in all innocence an offender against humanity. On the other hand, if he had no conscience, he would tell himself that the workers depended for their pittance upon the profitable investment of his thousands, write to his stockbroker, purchase shares in an oil-field or a palm-oil region, and expect the proletariat to be enthusiastic over, even to lay down their lives for, the extension and development of the Empire. . . . What the workers realise, and what the capitalist does not see, is that the last of the patriarchs, those who dominated the nineteenth century, were in an unnecessary hurry, that they put an intolerable strain upon their machinery and the men who tended it, and that, at last, they forced young men out to defend a system that had collapsed. The patriarchal or capitalistic system has not been broken by the European War. It had become antiquated a decade before that. Its knell was written by George Gissing in the 'nineties. The great Russians surveyed European civilisation with foreboding, knowing full well that their own people could never enter it until it had shaken off its patriarchal character. The Russians, ready to break through the evils of feudalism and serfdom, could not accept the slavery of industrialism with its triumph of mediocrity. The moral foundations of Europe had to be broken up before a revolutionary spirit could stir again in its civilisation. To avert the coming of the new age the patriarchs made war. They have brought on a premature birth, and plunged Europe into the throes of revolution before it was due, in the hope that their traditions may gain a new lease of life from the resulting confusion. It is the method of jealousy, and patriarchal institutions derive their power, and also their stability, from the smouldering passion of the jealousy with which the old regard the young. That endures from generation to generation, and ever the young of heart labour to overtake it and stamp it out; but it smoulders on beneath the surface, flares up, and destroys in a moment what years have gone to make, raises impassable barriers of heat, which yet are passed, though too much is spent in the effort; so that what is done falls far short of the dream. Old men in their jealousy contrive that the ways of life shall be so intricate that by the time a man has achieved the position and the experience to enable him to give the best that is in him, he too shall be worn and bitter and fearful of the young men coming after him. That is the beginning of patriarchalism, and Jehovah is made in the likeness of an old man whose thoughts and deeds spring from jealousy.

Two thousand years ago this time-hallowed jealousy was corrected by the saying, "God is love," and those two thousand years have been spent in a bloody anguish in the attempt to wrest the powers of the earth from the God of Jealousy for the God of Love. Jealousy in that anguish has been sweated out of the individual into the family, out of the family into the nation, and out of the nations into—what? Into rival Leagues of Nations, or is it shaken off for ever? . . . Russia has repudiated the patriarchs. It remains to be seen whether Labour in industrial civilisation will be strong enough to follow that example. Russia has had in Tolstoi, Dostoieffsky and Tschekov great preachers of love. The Western World has had Whitman, Gissing, Mark Rutherford, Romain Rolland, and, above all, César Franck. These, surely, are enough to give the inspiration that is needed in the crucial trial between jealousy and love, between evil and good, between the spirit that takes and gives nothing and the spirit that takes in giving. The last stronghold of that patriarchalism which grows out of jealousy is, by the irony which makes life even at its most tragic so charming, Great Britain, the "home of freedom." It is in Great Britain, the only-begetter of industrialism, that battle is joined, and it is in Great Britain that the battle will be won.

V

MARRIAGE

V

MARRIAGE

If society exists to protect human beings from their appetites, nowhere is the operation of society more imperative than with regard to that appetite which is so imperious that individual passions can produce general tragedies. If Cleopatra's nose had been shorter the face of the whole world would have been different. Through marriage the social contract touches the living core of humanity, and has its most direct influence upon the life of the generations. Unfortunately, marriage has been of all contracts the most lop-sided, because women have not been regarded as capable of entering upon the social contract. Woman could only have a relationship with the community through a patriarch, her father or her husband. Other communities, other laws, but hitherto all communities have agreed to keep women either in slavery or in tutelage, so that the contract of marriage has been everywhere a festering source of injustice and a denial of the spiritual equality from which the health of humanity springs, and until that equality is established here it is not likely to prevail anywhere else: for however well-meaning a man may be in his public character, he cannot act vigorously and freely if his private life is based upon injustice. Equality must exist in the home before it can appear in the life of the commonwealth, and men cry in vain for freedom so long as women are trammelled.

Marriage is a natural merger of two lives to create a holy state that is greater than either, and this state is fortified by daily habits and responsibilities. With the best will in the world a man and a woman in their relationship may fail to bring this holy state into being, and therefore no marriage has taken place. Churches and laws have evolved a system by which marriage is regarded as existing through patriarchal blessing, and they make no provision for dissolution in the event of failure, leaving it to daily habit and responsibility to preserve the tie. But when there is no spiritual bond the tie of habit is irksome and devastating.

Nature in her desire for reproduction cares

not a rap whether her couples are married or no, and of course society cannot emulate the indifference of Nature. But to society the spiritual creativeness of marriage is of even more importance than the production of children, and it is the spiritual principle of marriage that needs protection. By making a legal contract indissoluble, society denies that principle and commits self-injury through confusing a voracious appetite with a creative force. A mere appetite is easily sated, but a creative force will not desist until it has seen the farthest consequence of its actions. The one separates: the other binds. A man and a woman joined in a brief sensuality soon part in hatred, bitterness or contempt, or, worse still, in an indifferent nullity. If they happen by force of circumstances, or under a heated illusion—most frequently from pity on one side or the other—to have entered upon a legal contract, it is most cruelly anti-social to insist that they shall remain together through innumerable crises of nauseated reaction. It is worse than that: it is a degrading mockery which almost invariably leads to seeking relief in dissipation and adultery, to suffering for many innocent parties, and to the waste often of fine energies and qualities.

Society, while not emulating the indifference, should learn something from the largeness and generosity of Nature. Poor human beings struggling with their most overmastering instinct need all the succour they can gain from each other: they need far more than the patriarchal Thou Shalt and Thou Shalt Not. Very few are the men and women who are sunk so far in degradation that sexual gratification is become a light thing to them. Even the most idiotic lovers believe on the first impulse that it may be for ever; but unless love becomes a creative force with them it cannot endure. Men desire marriage because they do not wish to be plagued all their lives with dissatisfaction; but that dissatisfaction is only aggravated by a marriage that has failed, and, now that science has shown how intimately linked are the brain and the sexual apparatus in men and women, it is surely time that tyranny was removed from an element in society so vital to the happiness of its members.

A woman can no longer be regarded as a man's property. With that conception gone there is an end of the idea of marriage as a contract that cannot be reconsidered, and the legal and religious view of that contract has been rendered untenable by the artificial sterilisation of conjugation. A man and a woman married can no longer be regarded as delivered up to the mercies of their own fecundity. This, more than anything else, has contributed to the emancipation of women who now, as well as men, have a will in the matter. Until she had a will in the business of child-bearing a woman could not very well have a will in anything else, and to this has been due her subservience to patriarchalism and to laws made to protect her disabilities. The artificial sanction of marriage being removed, the natural sanction must be sought, and that sanction can only be found in the relationship of the parties themselves: a pragmatic sanction. A creative marriage will endure of its own deep satisfaction: a sterile marriage should be as easily dissoluble as any other form of partnership.

Ephemeral relationships between men and women, adultery and concubinage, exist and will exist whatever the law. It is right that the nobler relationship should be given honourable acknowledgment and treated, as indeed it is, as the basis of society, the guarantee of the home and the family; but relationships registered in mistake or under illusion should be subject to revision and dissolution, otherwise the standard of morality in the matter is degraded and the institution of marriage is called into contempt, and can be used, as indeed it too often is, for nefarious purposes, to gain money or influence, or to consolidate interests.

The institution of marriage, like—indeed even more than—anything else, has to be called in question now when we have to rid ourselves of everything that cramps our energies if we are to overtake the harm done by so many generations of moral indolence, which accepted the artificially established difference between the sexes, a tradition so ancient as to have won almost the sanction of a natural law. But with the increased division of labour the disabilities of women have been reduced almost to vanishing point, and their status has practically reached equality with men. Yet the laws and prejudices which govern marriage remain based upon the old inequality, and about no subject are prejudices so rampant.

This is because, as a rule, human beings cannot think of other people's love affairs without jealousy or disgust, and a scientific attitude towards sex is repulsive to the sentiment with which the subject is coated. Yet people who have to live scientifically in all other matters cannot afford to remain in ignorance or a state of inflamed distortion about the central passion of their lives. Men and women will no doubt lie to each other to the end of time, but if they lie with knowledge the game gains in piquancy and charm: and here hitherto women have had the advantage over men. They have of necessity been liars because they have known the truth, while men have been confused between lies and truth, and for this reason, as the laws relating to marriage have been made by men, they have remained muddled, ineffective, and are in a modern community a perpetual nuisance.

At present in Great Britain two people who have acknowledged the failure of their marriage can quite easily be divorced; but at the cost of degradation and unnecessary scandal, and the risk of a mess being made of their affairs by an incompetent or unscrupulous attorney. The one fatal bar to a divorce is the desire of the parties for it. Therefore the woman must perjure herself and swear that she desires the return of her husband, while the man must commit an open act of adultery. This method is pursued every day, yet a demand for the introduction of plain, simple honesty is met with cries of indignation, laments for the destruction and corruption of society, and denunciations of intelligent reformers as professors of license and abettors of libertinism: whereas, in fact, disgust for the operation of a divorce, drives many unhappy people to any lengths to avoid it, and they prefer to live in a veiled polygamy and polyandry with all the corruption of looseness added to the exasperation of secrecy. A society parched for honesty cannot afford to leave so rich a source of hypocrisy untouched. The trouble is that human beings are hypocrites and enjoy hypocrisy so long as it is profitable to them, and even after it has become injurious it is difficult to persuade them of the fact. Marriage being the profoundest of human relationships gives the greatest room for hypocrisy, and the more degraded it is the more room. A hard-and-fast law degrades marirage. If the parties to it cannot rescind an irksome contract, they have somehow to make it tolerable, and the easiest way of doing that is by lying to each other and resorting to the game of bluff, by which human affairs are for the most part conducted. But marriage is a more delicate affair than most. It is through marriage that men and women are in most immediate contact with humanity, and through humanity with the creative will, and as Russell Lowell put it—

> "You've got to git up airly
> Ef you're goin' to take in God."

Here most often the game of bluff breaks down and lives are wasted in years of barren suffering. Time may bring the tolerance of mute despair, but than this nothing could be more stultifying and sterilising to the human spirit which is at last through women everywhere in organised revolt. Laws made to protect women as property have to be amended in favour of laws to emancipate women as human beings, and with this change comes a fundamental alteration of the conception of property, the long overdue shift from ownership to trusteeship. Marriage also is a trust. Men and women are trustees for each other, and above all for the most sacred emanation of the human spirit, true wedded love, of which a child is the glorious symbol. No law is needed to protect this beauty, but only to protect those unfortunates who fail in its pursuit, and here again the difficulty is economic. Who is to protect the child that is only a child and not a symbol, and to see that the failure or the folly of its parents does not weigh too heavily upon it? Out of love a home will grow as naturally as a nest will grow out of the mating of birds. To clap a loveless man and woman into a joint existence is to breed disaster. Society is responisble for them as for all sufferers, and the immediate concern of society, which exists to abet the physical well-being of its members so that they may be free to pursue their spiritual welfare, is with the mother and the child, who in an ordered community might well be taken as the social unit, the home based upon true marriage being well able to take care of itself. By protecting the mother and the child society would be going far to save for marriage many unhappy people who are at present thrust out of it, and are, therefore, unable to contribute their keenest forces to the service of humanity. An immense amount of immorality could be saved by such a revaluation of moral ideas; and the division of women into two classes, those for pleasure and those for child-bearing, which so odiously grew up under the conception of women as property, would disappear, with the result that vast numbers of women would be released for work through which their sexual needs would be tamed. They would no longer be dependent for their career and their prosperity upon their sex. True marriage would remain untouched because it is unassailable. Those who defend indissoluble marriage do so out of their concern for the sanctity of property, and from their point of view they are right, for once the conception of marriage is elevated the conception of property must follow. If the moral code is lowered still further by an increase of legal tyranny and private license, then the value of property is heightened and economic tyranny gains in force. Human energy that is diverted from liberty creates tyranny. Conception, as Hamlet said, is a blessing, and there is no liberty without it. In true marriage each of the lovers is conceived and released by the other. So it is in all pure relationships into which love enters. That is love's activity, to conceive and bear liberty. If it is thwarted there is either barrenness or an abortion. Marriage is a principle which prevails everywhere and not only in the sexes. It prevails in the region of ideas, in art, in science, in politics, even in commerce. A bargain is a kind of marriage: fruitful if it be just and equitable, barren or abortive if it be dishonest. In all true work the principle of marriage prevails: the labourer is wedded to the earth, the craftsman to his materials, and the operation of this principle depends vitally upon its free working in the relations of men and women.

Society at present is very like the man in Swift, who on being informed that there was a mistake in the Bible, cried, "What! A mistake in the Bible? . . . Then I can go on with my drinking and whoring."—"What!" men seem to say, "kings and priests are just fools like ourselves; Tsars can be murdered and Emperors exiled! Then we can do what we damn please." And as what ignorant men please is generally to their hurt, it suits those who find patriarchalism profitable to encourage them in their doing, with the result that wealth, material and spiritual, is consumed, and things that were holy lose their sanction. But a greater book than the Bible has been opened, the Book of Nature, and a greater power than the wisdom of princes has been discovered, the heart of the people. Men are beginning to read the one and to honour the other, finding at last that the one true marriage is that between man and humanity. . . . It is for this reason that the words of governors appointed by years of intrigue are so vain and empty. Reforms can no longer be imposed from without in favour of a class who can see their advantage in it. Reform grows from within. Three generations of industrialism have created hideous abuses, but they have liberated man from the tyranny of the earth. In the struggle to achieve this the freedom of humanity has been conceived, and men will no longer submit to the tyranny of men. That was necessary until the tyranny of the earth was broken. It had its purpose and its sanction, but both are gone. Humanity aims higher now—to break first the tyranny of men, then the tyranny of the human mind, that the human spirit may at last know its freedom and live in unison with the creative spirit by whose will all that lives has its being.

Marriage, then, is symbolical of the greatest mystery. It is the fiery principle from which all other social principles emanate. It is the consummation of the social contract, the only begetter of liberty. How mistaken, then, is that view which would make it a clog upon the passions of men and women which only in liberty can find the coolness to reduce them to order! By suppression society deprives itself of that which it most needs: force and spontaneity, and defiles the social spirit at its source. By making the contract of marriage indissoluble, society robs men and women of the incentive to preserve the joy without which their relationship cannot endure. When joy goes nothing but the tie of money and habit is left. That may bind a tolerant affection, but that makes for stagnation, which is of all states the most injurious to society and the most blasphemous upon the principle of marriage. Yet it is the state most suited to the patriarchal system which brooks no questioning of authority, and sees it only in power. Most admirable from the point of view of that system are the innumerable streets in the innumerable cities of the world where life is stagnant; but from the point of view of the dwellers in those streets and those towns the outlook is very different. Their work is given back to them in a lie that every day grows more savourless: the pleasures they are allowed are thin and empty: marriage claps them into a little prison of a house and opens up to them no communal life: the delight they should expend in civic works and duties is diverted to vast undertakings directed by remote personages for which they have to pay in unintelligibly assessed taxes. In their own cramped lives they have to seek that which the ill-organisation of society denies them, and so perverse has that organisation become that it has arrived at a flat denial of the principle of marriage and aims at the use of the males for the purposes of war, of the females for breeding. Their mutual joy counts for nothing: this community, calling itself the State, ignores that and claims the little it has left under the pretext that it fears the designs and ambitions of other communities where the great mass of men and women are in much the same plight. Meanwhile the patriarchal system forbids communication between the communities, except through very narrow channels, and information about them is circulated in prejudicial sheets financed to maintain the system. Thus, as far as possible, by the system individuals and communities are kept apart, so that the world is like one vast cartel, a system by which huge firms are kept in competition and are only joined together by the fact that the same financiers extract profits from all of them. The patriarchs, in fact, have learned to profit even from feuds, so successful has been their usurpation. They keep humanity perpetually at war, whether with lethal or commercial weapons, so that nothing but profits are created. But humanity does not exist to create profits which are only a by-product. Humanity lives to release and create a spirit, and the time is coming when that purpose will be too strong for the patriarchs and their sycophants, who will stand convicted of mischievous futility; and society will then have its responsibility wrested away from them and diverted to the individual for whom the application of the principle of marriage in every walk of life is a necessity: for only through it can his conscience be kept alive, and society's only source of authority is the individual conscience expressing itself through the supple and efficient machinery of democratic control. If the individual conscience is suffered to exist there need be no fear of the religious and reverential emotions in men and women ceasing to be operative in human affairs. It is when that conscience is stifled that materialism becomes rampant and men become parasitic upon humanity. To a healthy conscience nothing is more abominable than a parasitic existence, and it is only because conscience is derided and defiled everywhere that the present extraordinary social system exists for the exploitation of mankind by man. With the past nearly exhausted the present generation, like its predecessor, has become parasitic upon the future, which must inevitably repudiate it and reassert the elementary principles that have been forgotten. The fantastic confusion of the present will fade from men's minds as they emerge into a clearer air, and in the huge effort to pay off the debts of their fathers they will learn that joy is won through persons and not through things; and that the denial of marriage leads to separation, and that separation leads to slavery.

The individual by himself is soon caught in his tyrannous desire: wedded to his beloved, be it a dream, a vision, a man, or a woman, he is one with humanity, and is sustained by a force that is unconquerable. The parasite upon humanity perishes of his own greed: the servant of humanity is master of the world, for all things yield up to him the treasure of their love, and join their creative will to his to make his life in sorrow and in delight a marriage song.

VI

WOMEN AS CITIZENS

VI

WOMEN AS CITIZENS

THERE are philosophers who can no more endure women patiently than they can the toothache, but they lack the indulgence to see that what they detest in women is not so much the brand of femininity as the mark of slavery. The dishonesty, the rapacity, the untrustworthiness, the shallowness, the ferocious egoism of women are those of all slaves who have no outlet for their passions save through their vanity, which is thus made to do the work of the will. The slavery of women has deprived men of their free companionship, with the result that they have been driven to make the brain do the work of the mind. Between the male brain and female vanity it is small wonder that a sorry mess has been made of human affairs, which have only been saved from irretrievable disaster by the fact that humanity as a species knows its business fairly well.

If their society is to be restored to sanity,

both men and women have to readjust their method of living and to discover a means by which, in public matters at least, they can understand each other, for while men think only with their brains and women with their vanity they must be hopelessly at cross purposes. (The men who, like women, think with their vanity are "sports," who, though frequently very successful, are insignificant.) As for life under modern conditions vanity is a less adequate equipment than brain, it is women who are first in moving towards a change, and making the discovery that the will only responds to the call of the mind. In their slavery they had accepted that men had a monopoly of mind; but when under industrialism their slavery became desperate, because their work was taken out of their hands, they had for a generation or two the leisure to consider the situation—the handiwork of man—and to find out that there was no mind in it whatever, and that such will as could be discerned was that of the species: no conscious will at all. The shock of it cracked the mirror of woman's vanity, and in her discontent she began to clamour for freedom, imagining that man was withholding it from her and not suspecting that she, by accepting slavery, was withholding it from man. Such has been the comedy of the sexes which the self-conscious generations have mistaken for a tragedy so profound that they have raised sex to the level of a taboo.

The development of self-consciousness into consciousness is the greatest effort of humanity for thousands of years, and it is perhaps from exhaustion after this effort that so many calamities are listlessly accepted as inevitable. The young equipped with a new consciousness do not know how to use it in a world still dominated by the old. They waste it in wild experiments and in intellectualising such experience as they can gather, though that is not much, as they are thwarted on every side by the remnants of self-consciousness, and their vision and sensations are so novel that they can find no guidance not even in the masterpieces of art of the ancient world. They find themselves more akin to the primitives and yet different from them. They have in living something of the joy of Heraclitus in philosophy, the exhilaration of being the first to do something. Their clucking is like that of the first hen to lay the first egg until they begin to wonder whether they are not after all the first egg. So absorbed have they been with their novelty that they have passed through the horror of the war almost as a matter of course, and it has become a screen between them and the old world. They are not irritated or provoked by the old people; they simply do not understand them, nor do they want to, except that they realise that the self-consciousness of the old must always have been a barrier between themselves and their lives. If the old people want power and pomp and sovereignty let them have them. . . . It is not only the intellectuals, the intelligentsia, who feel this, it is the young everywhere, intoxicated with their new consciousness and apt to despise intelligence, intellect, even imagination. Of course a great deal of their exhilaration is illusion, and they do not realise that a great deal of what they feel is the will of humanity asserting itself after ages of neglect, but they know that it is a force to which they can trust themselves absolutely, even through the direst misfortune. We are at the beginning of an age of faith, but it is different from its predecessors in that the faith will be conscious and critical, and fortified with knowledge and scientific methods of increasing and applying that knowledge. To the scientific study of the universe the young generation has gained the courage to add the scientific study of human nature. Without a conscious will the attempt would be in vain, but that has been gained, as will be acknowledged later, through the self-conscious sufferings of the preceding generations, but at present the gain seems like a miracle proceeding from some unimaginable source. It has as yet found no expression: it has been too intoxicating to leave room for more than living, but as it gathers soberness there is no doubt that it will be absorbed into an immense social effort. Seeking God through humanity it must first make humanity permeable, and destroy the conditions which make for denseness and stolidity. Already the intellectuals have accepted that as their task, and they set about it with something of the enthusiasm of the Americans for commerce and with much the same machinery, advertisement and a card-index. They are content to let the Americans be the bagmen of the world. They want to be its inspiration and to have that inspiration creeping through every cranny of society. Like people enamoured at first sight they are in love with love, but they want to understand love and to be conscious through every phase of it. They accept the sway not of emotions but of a will, and to that they devote their passions. Being conscious of the creative will in humanity they must, to preserve themselves, discover their own, and to that all their energies are attracted. Heroes and saints have lived like that in the past, but with bitter agony and suffering. The danger for the young of this marvellous time, this advent of an age of faith, is that they live so with such ease. They have no perplexity, hardly a shadow of doubt: there is so much that they can do without while the growing will broods within them, and they can smile happily at the desperate efforts of their elders to solve problems which do not need solution, because they will disappear when the new order begin to take shape and human beings become conscious in selection of what they want, instead of taking a hundred different things from life in case they should want one of them. . . . These young people are not possessive. They do not thrust upon each other what they have, but what they are. They turn to each other for confirmation of what they believe to be growing in themselves, and, finding it, they are reassured and smile happily and mysteriously. They exasperate their elders by leaving undone that which they ought to do, by doing in half an hour what has traditionally been done in a day, and by striking out in different directions every hour or so. They break every convention and many laws, but somehow they do not come to grief because they believe they are on the way to a world in which men and women will understand each other. They take understanding for granted, and even from the most unexpected and conventional persons it is forthcoming. Even the old are learning to appreciate the confidence with which the young face disaster, and to realise that it is a stronger power than calculation because it has no need to encroach on moral capital.

On the other hand, the confidence of the young is perhaps excessive. They have more to learn than they will admit, and they rely too much upon intellectual formulation. But whatever the tragedies their faults may bring about they will meet them face to face and not leave them to go dragging on through the generations. Their situation is such that they must do this, for they are charged with a direct responsibility to humanity: they have no church, no nation, no group to which their loyalty can be diverted. The powers of work at their disposal have broken down frontiers and barriers.

As women have had less to unlearn than men they are the more ready to assume this new citizenship that has been created out of the world's agony. Their desire for it, already awake before the catastrophe, is no longer thwarted by the institutions and prejudices of the old world, and they no longer need to waste energy in fighting as young men must against tradition, not to destroy it but to wring from it what is valid for the present and the future. Women, therefore, can bring into public affairs a freshness and eagerness of desire that have been far to seek, and they also bring into the open the secret knowledge of the ways of men which hitherto they have used to defend themselves. Men reveal themselves to women as they never do to each other, and with women admitted to the councils of humanity the need for a great deal of bluff and *blague* disappears. To a smaller degree the same is true from the other side, and the many little conspiracies of women drop out from the machinery of social intercourse. A big step has been taken towards collective honesty, which, like everything else collective, depends upon the necessities of the individual, which have been relieved more by the evolutionary raising of the status of women than by any other factor in the great development now in progress. To this more than to anything else is due the release of consciousness which has made it possible for humanity to turn from the exploration of the earth to that of human experience.

At the same time it has to be remembered that times of spiritual release bring great illusions which always receive the warmest welcome in the most eager minds, and it is likely that much of what women gain in freedom will be lost in self-deception, and their contribution to society may for a long time be thwarted by themselves as they gradually transfer their power of passionate concentration from individual human beings to humanity, but they themselves will make that easier as they bring to light the discomforts and crushing deprivations from which they have long suffered in silence. Above all, they will bring into the scheme of politics a care for children which has for too long been absent. Without that care it has been impossible to find any true orientation for public affairs, and no religion—because religions have kept women in subjection and used their power of devotion to create organisation—has been strong enough to make the Holy Family a valid symbol of worship. Religion has taken from society its most fiery force, the reproductive instinct, and spent it upon thin air. For the lack of it men have been working unsupported in a kind of void and have depended too exclusively upon the creative powers of men of genius, always too far ahead of their contemporaries to be able directly to serve them; so that, in fact, two societies have been created, one in which artists, prophets and seers have dwelt in equality, and another which is a spurious imitation of it in which men of action imitate the greatness without having the force of these others, and set up tyranny in the place of authority. A tyranny, even with the support of the greatest number, has no authority, and it is the tragedy of the nineteenth century that it followed Napoleon instead of Goethe. The glory of a Napoleon fades, while that of a Goethe increases in perennial fecundity; but the slave mind in its stunted ignorance is always so dazzled by a successful tyranny that it cannot see the light of authority, and women hitherto have been slaves, the slaves of a system even when they have gained the freedom of love. They are skilled in self-martyrdom, apt in immolation, acknowledging loyalty to husbands, lovers, or children; but blind to any larger loyalty, often bringing ruin when they seem most noble, because their virtues are that of the sham society which has imposed itself on the true, largely through their docile acceptance of the theatricality with which men have deceived themselves and falsified their values. That sham society has been like a film overlaying life, but with the immense movement of the soul by which women have gained a new status, the film has been broken and the light of authority set up by generations of work can shine through to the humblest life. Once it becomes clear that work is the only available authority it is apparent that circulation of work is to society what the circulation of the blood is to the human body, and as work has extended in its effects from community to community everything that impedes its circulation has to give way. Accordingly a system which attempted to confine women to their natural functions could not but break under that increasing pressure which demanded also the labour of women. It is the health-giving quality of work (as distinct from drudgery) that it makes the individual who does it insist that it shall be done upon honourable conditions, because a man or a woman can pocket his or her personal pride; but pride of work cannot be so summarily dealt with, for, consciously or unconsciously, it entails pride in humanity and establishes, perhaps, even more clearly than love, contact with the creative will. That contact is more living in women than in men through their child-bearing instinct, and when this is fortified with contact through pride of work a formidable power is released. Already under the old system there were common instances of this in the successful mother who was also house-proud. When women have in society the same pride that they have in the orderliness of the home, then they will not waste so much time as they do now in trying to understand the jargon with which for ages men have vainly been attempting to understand each other. Political economy should then receive the necessary corrective from domestic experience, and we might even be on the road to the evolution of a sound finance which would put an end to the old trouble of money that there is always too much of it or too little.

It must be in the experience of every married woman to have seen her husband's swagger ooze away as the pressure of their difficult relationship forced him into surrender to the inexorable fact that his success as a human being depends upon his success as a husband and father. Something like that has happened between the sexes in these crucial years. Men have been forced to face the truth that they and their handiwork depend upon their relationship with women. If that is false, so will be their doing. The upshot of this discovery is the further revelation that humanity is deeper than sex.

Women, one suspects, have known that all the time, and have worked through sex, while men have always been inclined to run away from it. The pity of it has been that women have not wanted anything much. They have bowed too humbly to the natural law which limits their fecundity to the thirty years between fifteen and forty-five, and have overlooked the fact that, while their maturity begins soon after twenty, that of a man does not begin until he has passed thirty, so that in any generation responsibility first falls upon the women. To that may be due some of the jealousy between the sexes, but if responsibility begins with the women of a generation it ends with the men, and both need the support of the other.

Recognition of these facts, points, like that of other salient facts, to education as the solvent of the difficulty and as the road leading from a congested existence to a free life. The education of the last fifty years was necessitated by the recognition of the facts adduced by science working upon the phenomena of Nature. The facts revealed by the operation of science upon human nature necessitate a new phase of education, which must take its character from the new needs of women as citizens and break away from the traditions that have grown out of the education of men rooted in religion, which, drawing its sustenance from the captivity of women, has no more to give to humanity. The price of material progress and physical adventure was the subjection of women. That price has been paid in full, and the desire and the will of humanity is for spiritual adventure, and the price of that is the price of liberty—eternal vigilance. That, in every generation, as we have seen, begins with the women and ends with the men, and both must be trained for it, and their training is the first charge upon the efforts of humanity.

It is true that defence comes before opulence, but the only defence of humanity is education, for without that one generation will always defend itself at the cost of the next in defiance of justice and to the lasting injury of liberty. To the present generation these truths have been brought home in bitter fashion, and the young women of to-day entering upon citizenship are vigilant in their guard of the freedom they have won, not only for themselves, but also for men who could never be free while their efforts were based upon the subjection of those who should be most deeply their companions. With the needs of women ennobled by freedom, those of men become subject to fundamental emendation: the need of wisdom is increased, that of physical wealth reduced, since a man must henceforth win by his character that respect which hitherto has been too easily given to his property. With women no longer property the value of property diminishes, the conceptions based on it lose their force, and socially influence becomes a greater thing than power. No man with force or economic pressure at the back of his mind can utter the true word which again and again in history has shown itself mightier than force; and it is by the true word that henceforth humanity must be governed, because the violence of men reacts always to their own hurt. With women entering upon citizenship violence receives a check, and the untruth with which it is excused and maintained will be speedily reduced to absurdity by the art learned by women in their slavery of supporting male fictions even after the need for them has ceased, until, without a word, they are exposed. Life is a comedy, and it is tragic only in so far as men and women fail at crucial moments to summon up the vitality necessary to meet them. Then the conventions break, passions snap control, and the brutality of human nature for a time holds sway. On the whole women are better comedians than men, more tenacious, tougher and more courageous; and even as slaves they have been marvellously acute in giving men what they want rather than what they think they want. These powers of theirs have hitherto been confined to the family, but the family has been absorbed into the industrialised community, which, for lack of making a proper use of women, has come to grief. The omission is being repaired. The advent of women as citizens releases men for further and higher adventures, which, properly directed, should make the world a place greater than was ever dreamed of by those who, as feudalism fell away into the past, strove to mark out for humanity the direction of its destiny.

The gentleness of women is largely a male fiction. They have a ferocity and a hardness which, turned in the right path, are the very qualities needed for breaking through the confused thoughts and emotions which are humanity's legacy from the misfortunes of the past. Their experience has made them realistic, perhaps a little cynical and suspicious of the too easy idealism in which men have been accustomed to take refuge. Above all, they know only too well that bills have to be paid, and that recklessness in public affairs reacts fatally upon the price of food. They know that before anything else is attempted, children must be fed and clothed. They are the last to emerge from feudalism, and they should bring into the new society something of the spirit that animated the old, something of the pride that built in every community a house of God and made it nobler than any house built for man. It is for lack of this that communal buildings in the modern world are so ignoble. They are built only to serve the practical needs of men without reference to their service of a power greater than themselves, without which—so nicely adjusted are the laws of humanity—they cannot gain even their own advantage. Women serving the family have that ingrained in them, and, turned to the service of humanity, they will gain the support of humanity's creative will. Theirs is the power, theirs should be the desire, and with them rests the immediate responsibility for the fate of the next few generations. With them largely rests the task of rebuilding society from the bottom up, so that when the superstructure collapses, as it inevitably must, there shall remain a finer edifice. While the new society is built we have to dwell in the ruins of the old. The important thing in society is not political institutions, but the lives of the millions of workers which go on much the same whatever happens. It is out of them that the communal life grows, and it will be the first duty of women to see that the new communal life is not divorced from them as the old has been, and most probably the first field of their energies will be the schools which have to be reclaimed from the old communal life. That is the key to the reorganisation of social machinery. Reclaim the schools and the rest follows. Every village, every parish, should have a school in which it can take a pride as the institution through which the community acknowledges its responsibility for the children, who, after the first few years, need more than their parents can possibly give them. With the community accepting responsibility, the parents are then released to achieve a greater fulfilment of their lives than if they are crushed by the burdens imposed on them by the exercise of their natural functions. Again, it cannot be too often repeated that the purpose of society is to save men and women from being overwhelmed by their responsibilities. Society, indeed, has grown out of the pooling of responsibilities, and again it must be repeated that its sole sanction is work. The release of women has come about through their being deprived of the work imposed on them by the feudal family. They have claimed and won the right to contribute their work, over and above the bearing and care of children, to the industrial community. With their victory ends the close division of humanity into nations; and humanity has entered upon a phase when it can be acknowledged, practically as well as ideally, that the industrial community and it are one. Women then must either be citizens of the world or slaves; and if they meet the latter fate, with them the whole will dwindle away from its destiny and the races will have entered upon the process of disintegration.

Coming fresh to citizenship, it is likely that women may be able to supply that civic sense which is so painfully lacking in the organisations of Capital and Labour, both of whom—naturally enough in a competitive state of society—aim at getting as much as ever they can for their women and children to secure them against poverty. Remove poverty and you remove the necessity for organisation against it. Organisation can then be used for fruitful purposes. Women who are used to being supported may remove from the male mind the objection to the idea of it. Every human being is, in fact, supported by humanity, but it has been the custom to ignore that fact. Admit it and there can come into social thought the simplification which scientific discoveries have brought about in philosophy. The refusal to admit it, the jealous preservation of sovereignty is the chief stumbling-block in the way of the unification of society. Women have a certain skill in painlessly picking obstinate ideas out of the minds of men, who often cling to them out of an unnecessary chivalry. Let it be so now and the world will be immeasurably the gainer.

Above all, women are subject to psychic storms which clear the air, become fouled and poisonous wherever human beings are gathered together. The brooding thought of women breaks in them and fertilises the seeds of thought in men, bringing forth what else remained concealed, or covered up in unconsciousness. Many a woman, even where she could not understand, has counted her life well lived because she was once the occasion of some germination in the soul of a man. It is among the profoundest needs of a woman and gives her her most subtle powers. Let them be used for the community, as they must when women begin to live socially, and a great source of power that is now almost entirely wasted can give its energy to the working of the whole.

It becomes clear, then, that men and women must more and more be allowed to govern themselves, to create and adapt the machinery they need for the satisfaction of their requirements, and that social philosophy must advance to this from the idea of getting out of men and women as much as possible for as little as possible. There is no reason why, in time, society should not be as supple and as varied as life itself, giving back an hundredfold the work that is put into it.

VII

SCIENCE AND ART

VII

SCIENCE AND ART

As old sanctions and authorities pass away hasty attempts are made to replace them, but with the crumbling of institutions there is an end of the ideas by which they were sustained. As small communities are merged in larger, and the single human community appears to view, it becomes clear that it has always existed, and that it has been supported, though all others were unfaithful, by the thinkers, who have been to all appearances a community apart, doing its work unrecognised and yet unconsciously honoured in the homage, usually posthumous, paid to great men, who, being of all human beings the most human, have met the ironic fate of being treated as demi-gods and given a reverence of the kind accorded to potentates, though nothing could be farther from the recognition of their seeking, since they, of all men, have understood and practised democracy and co-operation when other workers were lost in the mazes of competition. There has always been an international community, for the imagination overleaps the barriers set up on the ways of common trade, and there is no property in ideas round which jealous defences can be set up. Confucius and Kant work together, regardless of the frontiers of time and place, and they work together as all men should for humanity. It has always been so and always the discoverers have been opposed by those whose profit seems to lie in thwarting change and readjustment, but though jealous communities are composed and decomposed, theirs persists as the grand model which humanity through all its upheavals must emulate. Here, then, is a community inspired by the authority of work, and it has always put all other authorities to shame, and has, indeed, been stronger than any code of law ever devised; but from the minds of the great mass of men its existence has been concealed, and thinkers and artists have always been presented to them as isolated wonders, creatures almost of another sort, though their sole privilege has been a greater sensibility to the tides that move in humanity. Here, then, in works of philosophy, art, music, is the authority that is needed.

With the single community acknowledged, the workers in science and art can follow their calling in the open, and so soon as the Law, devised to protect property, is adapted to the protection of work, they will be able to establish what is lacking now—direct contact with the lives of common men—and no longer be dependent upon the caprices of politicians. This does not mean that government should be handed over to the artists and scientists. Government and authority are two very different things. The work of the artists and scientists is the maintenance of authority without which there can be no good government. Truth has to be re-stated for every generation, for no two generations speak the same language. In the decaying years of feudalism government usurped the position of authority, and that usurpation has to be removed. It can only be done in one way, and that slowly, by education, that is by helping the people to understand such truth as is revealed to them. A great discoverer is unintelligible to his contemporaries, but it is always possible for them to appreciate the tradition that has made his work possible. The tradition of science and art is a far greater thing than any national tradition, and it is in this that children should be educated, for without understanding of the greater there can be no true appreciation of the less. If, for instance, there was ever a true King of England his name was William Shakespeare; and President Wilson, in speaking nobly for America, is the mouthpiece of Walt Whitman. The destiny of humanity is shaped by vision, not by Law, which should be the means by which the vision is expressed in daily life. Laws which subserve the purposes of temporal power thwart the operation of vision and injure daily life, lead to the destruction of imagination, and blight the hopes of the future. Vision and the pressure of daily life lead slowly to inventions which the generations are apt to regard as their sole unaided work, but, as we have seen, no work is unaided, all work is done in common, and all work depends upon that of the community of artists and scientists, where there is emulation but no competition. The spirit of competition, which is so ardently defended by those whose fortune depends on it, is the outcome partly of jealousy, partly of the cruel system by which a man is solely responsible for his wife and family. That system has been overthrown by the insurrection of women, and a new system of common responsibility is coming into being. In the community of artists and scientists that system has always prevailed, since without acceptance of it nothing can be done. Artists and scientists are allied in defence of the human spirit as expressed in ideas: following their example all men should be joined together in their work in defence of that spirit as expressed in flesh and blood. The system is the same, only the medium is different. Without system nothing is accomplished, and without consciousness of tradition no truth can be revealed. Unity can only be achieved through devotion which is native to every human heart. The pity of it is that so few have the courage of it, but by the revelation of the community of science and art that can be fortified, and men can be given what they most need: the sense of serving something beyond the purpose immediately before them. That sense has in Europe been monstrously abused by the doctrine of the sovereign state, which has been suffered to absorb into itself both the sovereignty of the individual and the sovereignty of humanity, which are the two shining principles of the community of the artists and scientists. Without them life is reduced to nonsense, and the blind instinct of humanity has wasted four years and millions of lives in attempting to destroy it—in the wrong way. A perversion that has grown through generations cannot be destroyed in a moment, and it certainly cannot be removed by the exhaustion of the young life which is its natural enemy, yet, though the waste has been disproportionate, there has been this much gained: that the perversion is revealed for what it is, and the distortion of society through it has become patent. Nowhere is this more so than in the quarrel to which it has given rise between the brain-workers and the hand-workers of the world, revealing the hideous fact that for two or three generations the executive brain-work of the world has been neglected, owing to the ease with which, on paper, satisfactory results could be obtained by leaving it to the automatic working of commercial and social machinery. The complaint of the hand-workers is just. They have been as grievously betrayed by the executive brain-workers of the world as ever the peasants of the feudal system were by the barons, priests and kings who swindled them in the name of religion. The brain-workers have exacted vast payment for work that they have left undone, and the burden laid upon the industrial millions is intolerable. They in their ignorance imagine despairingly that they must take unto themselves the brain-work for which they are so ill-equipped. They know perfectly well that men and classes who have lost the habit of work cannot regain it; and they do not know where to turn, because they are unaware of the community of artists and scientists who, through all the abuses of society, have kept alive the principle of loyalty to the human spirit. Between the hand-workers and that community stands everywhere the indolent class which knows no loyalty. Meanwhile to defend themselves the hand-workers have thrown up their own brain-workers to protect them as a class against the depredations of the indolent and irresponsible, whose economic status gives them so devastating a power; but without the authority of art and science these brain-workers also cannot but become predatory, and becoming so they will cease to work. That is inevitable in any community in which work is not gradually refined until it flowers naturally and beautifully in art. Without such gradual refinement art becomes a plaything. Indeed, art has only flourished when by accident a community has for a time achieved this condition through some fleeting inspiration. There are always, and always will be, loyal workers in art to keep its tradition alive, but achievement depends upon the health of the community, which cannot always be measured by external events. There are obstacles which genius cannot surmount.

The hand-workers of the world are aware that more than material comfort has been withheld from them. They know that economic justice alone cannot satisfy them. They know that the truth of their generation has been kept from them. They are beginning to perceive that just as their work was on the point of breaking through national boundaries those boundaries were strengthened, and that the wealth that should have removed them was used to turn them into battlefields, and they know that life has become as barren as those burned and scarred areas. It is welling up in their minds that only brain-work can repair this monstrous damage, and that they are in the hands of people who cannot use their brains, people incapable of suffering, egoists, unhappy, inert; and they are realising that these people are the boundaries which they have been urged to defend. The earth on one side of a river is the same as that on the other; the two sides of a mountain reach to the same summit, but the people may not reach the summit because they may not trespass on the pleasure-grounds that bask in the sunlight of the slopes. They have been taught that art also is a pleasure-ground on which they may not trespass, and this is the most shameful lie of all. They have been led to think that science is a darkness and a menace from which they must keep their eyes averted, and they have behind them generations of the habit of docility; but, once it becomes plain that they are separated only by the inertia of a few thousand people, then energy will leap in them to ally their labour with that of the artists and scientists, where alone they can find the brain-work without which they cannot find escape from the dishonourable condition thrust upon them by the incompatible alliance of honest work and commercial cunning which at present governs humanity.

The split, then, is between honesty and dishonesty, the growing decency of private life and the increasing corruption in public affairs. Assertive nationalism in vain attempts to conceal the true nature of the division, and the fact that behind the demand of the hand-workers are imperishable moral principles and the insistence of the human conscience upon the social contract. There may, there probably will, be compromise, but the outcome will be, consciously or unconsciously, an admission that humanity is greater than any portion of it, and some glimmering of the truth that artists have maintained ever since the human mind was kindled by the glow that comes from work honestly and honourably carried out. That is the sole light in our darkness. Love contains no other illumination. The task of science and art is simply to increase that light, that understanding may increase to bring to greater perfection the marriage of the inward beauty of the soul with the overwhelming beauty of the universe. Without such marriage men and women are overcome, their passions smoulder away and are never fully used in the service to which in their birth they are dedicated. They remain the victims of fear, and are only allied to their fellows in panic, when they should be continuously joined in devotion.

There is much lamentation over the decay of religion in the industrial community; but religion that denies art and science must decay, because it attempts to deny Man's approach through humanity to the highest mysteries, as if any other way were open to him. The religious impulse awakened and yet given no channel simply reacts in misery, for it springs from the instinct of love and is creative, and cannot rest content with expression in an act of vacant worship. Prayer clarifies the soul for action—as the soul understands action, swift, direct, yet patient and indomitable; but if the mind be darkened the soul is impeded and doomed to disappointment. Art and science, being work at its highest, bring the only available illumination to the darkened mind, and a religion which denies them deprives all other work of its illuminating power and leaves the soul dependent upon the fitful fire of the passions. Action then becomes spasmodic and unintelligible, discouraging and baffling rather than inspiring, and the soul gains no strength but gradually weakens, and the burden of humanity is increased. How cruel, then, is it for religion, pretending to care for the soul, to deprive it of its only sustenance; and what miseries, what disasters does it prepare through its arrogance! Art was once the handmaid of religion, but art fortified by science is denied by the institutions to which religion has given birth. In the education grudgingly allowed by those institutions to the people, art and science are cunningly divorced, and neither is held up in honour. The result is, that education has debauched the innocence of the people's minds. The ignorance of the peasant is transparent compared with the opaque fog in the minds of the town-dwellers, and this fog reverts upon the heart; stultifying the emotions so that individuality and spontaneity are lost, and the word Education means a thing cursed rather than blessed. Science is exploited to bring material comfort and wealth, never to spread knowledge: art is not suffered to bring spiritual ease nor to fortify imagination. Knowledge and imagination are denied in favour of the assimilation of unco-ordinated facts as the only mental process suffered to operate in social existence. It is small wonder, then, that a need is discovered for discipline, but if it is made impossible for the individual to discipline himself it cannot be achieved by any external agency. A habit of obedience in public affairs may be inculcated, but against that the private person is mutinous, and finds stealthy relief in personal disloyalty, in deception, slackness and an increasing inability to distinguish between truth and falsehood, and finally a definite preference for ugliness over beauty, and with that of falsehood over truth. The streets, the newspapers, of any modern town betray the prevalence of this condition in the minds of men, vitiating their capacity for service and their aptness for the democratic form of society in which the efforts of their forefathers have made it possible for them to live. Without a drastic change they will only be able to exist in it, disloyal both to the past and the future.

It is said in extenuation that this is a scientific age, and that science is not concerned with beauty but with facts. That is not true. Without the illumination of intellectual beauty facts cannot be discovered. They remain concealed behind the mists of illusion. The beauty served by the scientist is not that served by the artist, but it is akin to it, and the spirit of their service is the same. The discoveries of science are used with no sense of service, and therefore do not take with them the spirit that produced them: the shadow is taken, and the substance is left, for in all human things the spirit is the substance. The discoveries of science have been gulped down in such haste that the industrial generations, like a greedy dog, have had to vomit them. Bare facts are an unwholesome diet, and, indeed, are only palatable in an artful concoction, as we are beginning to find to our cost, so that art from being an epicurean diversion has become a practical, indeed a hard necessity. Religion has been discarded: facts have been found an inadequate substitute, and it is slowly dawning on our numbed intelligence that it was not the discoveries of science that mattered, but the brave and adventurous spirit: just as it was not the discoveries of Columbus, Drake and Cook that made them great, but the spirit in which they went forth on uncharted seas. That brings forth fruit an hundredfold in the power to use their discoveries. As with the explorers of the earth, so with the explorers of the forces that animate it, and both need the support of the explorers of human experience. Without moral discovery no noble use can be made of the powers placed in our hands by physical and scientific adventure, for of all work the bravest and the hardest is that of the artist, and it is from that work that the light of authority shines most brightly. Both art and science repudiate economic power as firmly as they have done religion as a firm basis for human existence, and economic power, like religion, has perished in the wars of its own creation. Men fight when they feel the ground giving way beneath their feet. The sickening dread that fills them darkens their minds and infuriates their senses until, despairing of higher aims, they remember primitive satisfactions which surge through the memory and drive them mad, and when the madness leaves them they are brought face to face with the fact that these satisfactions have lost their potency. Men of heart, men of imagination know this, and are driven to labour in art and science hoping always to overtake the despair creeping in the veins of their fellows: always hitherto in vain, because the pleasure or the power created by their efforts has been kept by the few from the many. That systematic deprivation should be nearing its end. The artists and scientists are the aristocracy, without which democracy cannot exist, that is, they live in a democracy which transcends death and time, and makes possible a democratic society in an existence limited by time and death. In a healthy community this is acknowledged by the maintenance of public galleries, libraries, theatres, concert halls, universities; but in an unhealthy society the communal force of art is ignored, and science, except in so far as it is profitable, is flouted lest the people should discover in themselves the secret of freedom, and begin to perceive that he who turns his work into drudgery for higher wages loses more than he gains: by self-exploitation increases the tyranny of the economic system, by that increase inflates prices, and meets in the end that very trouble of insufficient means which he designed to avoid.

Self-exploitation is a definite act which in a modern community every worker is forced to commit under the menace of starvation. The community of artists and scientists is democratic precisely because it is impossible for the workers in it to exploit themselves. If they do so they cannot achieve art or science. The revolt of the hand-workers is against self-exploitation. The strength of their organisations gives them breathing-space in which to realise that if they had not to commit this act they could not be exploited by the classes who have betrayed them. Directly they assert the right to contribute their work freely to any undertaking, they will be able to break the vicious circle, and to let in authority as the ruling principle which will quickly reveal to them the fact that the democracy of art and science is the heart of humanity from which its life-blood, work, flows as mysteriously and as easily as the vivid stream in the human body. The sustenance taken from the earth turns in the body to blood, in society to work. The principle is the same, and it should dominate the great organisations now being formed to give men the strength to add the conquest of themselves to their victory over Nature.

VIII

SOCIAL STRUCTURE

VIII

SOCIAL STRUCTURE

MEN are rather like beavers building dams which the flood of life continually washes away, and one dam is very like another. Possibly beavers, like men, believe that every dam will be permanent, for no other reason than that they, wonderful creatures that they are, have built it. Men also, like beavers, are amphibious, but in different elements. There may have been a time when men also were aware only of earth and water, but slowly they have learned to live both in life and in certain intimations of immortality, though too often with a pathetic confusion between the two. However, the amphibious capacity is there, and has to be acknowledged in any philosophical speculation. In the individual the dual element is accepted as a necessary condition of being, but in combination for social purposes the intimations of immortality are generally ignored as providing an undue complication. Unfortunately for society, it is a fact that only through his intimations of immortality can a man use his senses effectively, and if he attempts as a social being to dispense with them he is as maimed as if he had lopped off his legs. This power rightly to use the senses comes from the memory of humanity, of which every man according to his constitution has a greater or less share. It is commonly called genius, and is honoured in those who, contrary to the prevailing habit, have the courage of it, and, as shown in the last chapter, have alone the capacity for constructing an enduring society simply because they retain their strongest social instinct. Nearly every individual retains enough to keep himself sane, but not enough to preserve the sanity of society. It is selfishness, if you will, inability to learn that the self is best served by being disinterested, but men are not disinterested chiefly because they find that no one is expected to be so. The most remarkable quality of human nature is its capacity for doing and being what is expected of it.

If, therefore, we desire to construct a sane society, the first step in that direction is to raise the world's expectations of human nature. Indeed, that is what has been gradually happening, through history. The more things change the more they are the same, but the more they change the more we recognise the wonderful possibilities latent in them. Increasing recognition is progress.

No one expects miracles, but every one now expects the social instinct of the race to make hay of human theories. By identifying the social instinct of the race with genius in the individual, a glimmering of order begins to show through the chaos, and the amphibious character of humanity becomes socially a strength instead of a weakness. It is possible then to reconcile human nature with Nature, and to see that a great deal of the social insanity of the past has been due to human insensibility and lack of power really to assume superiority. Nature retains earthquakes, thunderstorms, violent seas, poisonous insects, putrefaction and other agencies with which to disturb human organisation, which, however, has given the individual power to emancipate himself. It remains to be seen whether or no he has won that emancipation at the cost of being enslaved by organisation, but even if that has happened a few generations should bring liberation from that also.

Organisation is all very well for physical needs, but to satisfy the social instinct structure is needed. Organisation has dug out and built admirable cellars, but the edifice itself has not yet begun to appear, and no one wants to go on indefinitely living in cellars, however comfortable they may be. A man, especially a woman, must have pride in the dwelling-place, and the stronger the social instinct the greater the pride.

The factory system is the cellar in which human beings of the twentieth century are called on to live, and no one takes any pride in it, though men do undoubtedly take pride in the machines, the huge dynamos, the vast printing machines, the marine turbines, the twelve-cylinder aero-engines, with which they work, but they desire also an equal pride in their own lives. Why should more and more energy go into machines and less and less into the lives of men and women? Why should the available amount of happiness so alarmingly shrink, and the dwindling thoughts of men move in an increasing chaos? It is small wonder that the social instinct has taken alarm and begins to insist that some noble edifice shall be raised on so formidable a ground plan.

The Russians, who enjoyed the doubtful privilege of living in a dilapidated mediæval structure, have razed it to the ground, and start level with the rest of us. There are only two Emperors left in the world, the Emperor of India and the Emperor of Japan. The workers of the world have their grand opportunity to unite, but they do not, because, though the will is there, they have no plan, no scheme, not even a rough draft committing their dream to paper. Their dream, like the society in which they have suffered so long, is formless, and they know not what to build. They are hand-workers and they have to build a house not made with hands. Fortunately, they have the habit of work, and are humble enough to be willing to learn as they go along, letting their past sufferings be the instructors of their future hopes. Their care, as always, will be for their children, and in building for them they should create the model that future generations must follow.

Imagine a school that should satisfy the love of a mother for her child, instead of a place to which a child is torn to satisfy a grudgingly made law. The difference is one of spirit, but the question here is all of such difference, between the new and the old. . . . Such a school in any village, any parish, should have about it the communal pride that has fallen away from the Church. It would be a place of simplicity, health and beauty, with playgrounds, gymnasium, laboratory, workshop, a clinic, a garden with allotments and a play-room, with a properly equipped stage for the regular production and performance of plays, so that the children should learn the right use of their hands, brains and imaginations; and the teachers should be given a status equivalent to the authority vested in their sacred calling. No smaller word will serve: their calling *is* sacred, because it gives its practitioner access to the human mind at its most delicate and susceptible, when if it be not approached tenderly and with reverence it will surely sustain injury. The reverence of the teacher for his calling should inspire respect for his craft and all that it implies of good or ill for humanity.

In such a school should be the beginnings of democracy, the children being responsible for its organisation, with reference, if need be, to their parents, whose work, after all, pays for it. With such a training in practical democracy they could as they grew proceed to the factory with some equipment for its application there, and from that their capacity could work in their union, their parish, or municipality, and so up through the larger units of social organisation. They would very quickly learn to apply democracy to the home where it is most needed, and in this way the new spirit would find its way through the whole of human society. Without the release of that spirit, nothing can be done and nothing will be achieved, but a dreary levelling out in which the duality of human nature will be denied more bluntly than ever. Equality and fraternity are fine ideals for the one element of human nature, but the other, brooding on its immortality, insists upon the aristocratic privilege of privacy, or, in one word, Liberty. It is the lack of privacy that makes poverty so devastating a thing, more deadening and stultifying even than the fear of actual want. A man becomes a healthy social being by dint of the continual gymnastic of sacrifice, and if he has nothing to sacrifice he cannot enjoy or profit by the exercise. Rob a man of his privacy and you strip him of his power to develop the social instinct that is native to him. He becomes, whatever his prosperity, a burden to himself and, whatever his wealth, a drudge who cannot become a worker. Which a man is to be, drudge or worker, is settled very early in life; and it is very largely to escape the material penalties of drudgery that social cunning has been developed to so fine a pitch, and that has meant the condemnation to drudgery of numbers that increase alarmingly from generation to generation, and with that a weakening of the impulse to give form and structure to society and a barricading of the indolence which takes and gives nothing, and corrupts the only structure that we have, Finance.

There is no valid objection to the use of money as a symbol for work, except that it is not regarded or respected as a symbol, but is treated as a commodity like any other of which any man is entitled to as much as he can lay hands on without infringing the law. But money is different from other commodities in that it exists by social agreement as a means of maintaining the currency of work—in which commodities are included as the result of work and therefore part and parcel of it. Breach of that agreement is a breach of honour, and any shuffling of money which does not transfer work from individual to individual, or from group to group, is an injury to society of the same kind as that which accrues from the hoarding of money for its own sake. Both these offences will always exist, but the time is passing when they could be regarded as virtues, for the time has arrived when the financial structure of society must be drastically altered, so that all accumulations of work or money can be democratically used and democratically controlled.

Words by reiteration lose their meaning, but very often differences of meaning can be composed after the passage of time. For three generations now the words Capital and Labour have been used in such sharp opposition to each other that they are generally accepted as being irreconcilable, and in ordinary intercourse words replace the facts they should mean in the minds of speaker and hearer. Capital is Labour, or work, kept in storage. It has been cruelly abused by the custom of treating labour as a purchasable commodity. The labourer contracts to give his work in exchange for its equivalent in money, which represents work in storage. The bargain should be between equal men on equal terms, but it is hard for the labourer to forget that his forefathers were serfs, and for the capitalist to shake off the idea that the men in whose place he stands were noble lords, and by divine right owners of men as they were owners of cattle. But for the refusal of the capitalist to do his share of the fundamental brain-work of the world the labourer might even now agree not to remember that he is a free man, at any rate in theory. But the betrayal remains, and with it the sore suspicion that it has created. More than material discontent is at work, and the hand-worker seeks in the brain-worker not a master, but a colleague. There the artist, whose master is the human spirit, joins hands with him; the two workers, who have always sought each other, come together to their mutual relief, and together they can proceed on their healthy task of simplification. The artist's whole being cries: Simplify, simplify, because without simplicity there is no art: the artisan from his experience knows shrewdly that without simplicity there is no life. If emotions are complicated it means that they have come to the surface before they are ripe. If the problems of every day become hopelessly complex it means that some one somewhere has been in a hurry. Every worker knows that if he gets too far away from his work he loses his touchstone, and makes blunders impossible in his normal existence; and every worker knows that if by ill-luck he finds himself among people to whom work is as foreign as the poles, he suffers from such a twisting and torturing of life into uncognisable shapes as out of Bedlam he could never have imagined —a noise, a nervous tremor, a shattering of social intercourse into fragments and a maddening syncopation of the rhythm of life. In a state of society in which it is a legitimate ambition to avoid work, that oppression hangs everywhere like a damp mist, making a rust upon the machinery of society and an ague in the bones of the men who live in it, and the energy to remove these impediments can only come from the release of the inward light of the soul. Those who are content to live in a dead and decaying society must themselves be dead and decaying, morally lost; and people in that condition will only respond to economic pressure, which by a just dispensation always follows on the disasters they induce by their indifference. There is a limit to the extent to which one generation can live on the efforts of its predecessors and on mortgaging those of its successors. An actuary might estimate it, but long before it is reached the conscience of honest men begins to protest, and if their protests are not heeded the result is, as a rule, either war or revolution, or both.

It is doubtful whether war or revolution can be avoided, but it should be possible to build a social structure which is proof against them. First, the foundation must be solid. The foundation is the rough work of the world, and that can only be made solid if it is done in honourable conditions: that is, if it is organised upon an equitable contract between the brain-workers and the hand-workers, with a properly appointed authority to act as trustee between the two. The Japanese build houses which are proof against earthquake by transmitting the shock of the disturbance to a pendulum. In the social structure the pendulum is public opinion, which, when the authority of the democracy of the artists and scientists is established—as it can be by education—should swing so freely and with such momentum as to defy manipulation. The point is that public opinion, to be of service instead of disservice, must depend upon such honesty as human nature has achieved. To be honest, as this world goes, is to be one man picked out of ten thousand. Rascality cannot be obliterated, but it can be curbed; no longer by the threat of punishment in Hell, but by a swifter painful reaction than is possible in the present scheme of things, under which men live in such enormous units that the consequences of their doings take too long to reach them, and by the time the effect of one rascality reaches the doer, another can be accomplished as a defence against it. The consequence is that the effects of rascality accumulate and break into disaster involving the innocent and the guilty alike, and the unsuspecting innocent more deeply. That is why contemplation of the present order of society inspires such disgust. It may feed and clothe the people more efficiently than any previous system owing to its vastly improved transport, but it huddles them together, deprives them of privacy, and, therefore, of liberty, and passes on to the most helpless the consequences of all ill-doing.

We are not looking for a Utopia in which all men shall enjoy a perfect happiness. It is not happiness that makes a society healthy so much as the striving for it; and the complaint here brought against a world of communities which deny the existence of a single human community is that it cramps striving. and without that the work of the world suffers. When that happens rascality thrives, which is what Dr. Johnson meant when he said that patriotism is the last resort of scoundrels. There are, however, honest patriots to whom the idea of a single community is repellent, for it corresponds in their minds to a dream of an anonymous and amorphous mass of human beings without colour or character in their lives. But a man loses character in proportion as he transfers his pride in being a man to any lesser element of his being. When men are men first, and Englishmen, Frenchmen, Germans afterwards, there can be some hope of their acknowledging the most characteristic product of their nationality, its art. Men cannot detach themselves from their own racial experience, but they can, with a very little knowledge, learn to respect that of other men, and with the community of art before them, they can begin to admit its truth into their daily activities. With that the growth of the social structure can be seen, and some element of design can be introduced into it, for design is born out of the consciousness of the human mind of the rhythm and impulse of humanity, most easily felt in love, most purely apprehended through work.

The attempt to build the social structure after the designs laid down by theology from the roof downwards has failed. A roof is well for the body, but the soul needs no other than the sky. The social structure, then, must be builded to the heavens, as science is built, and poetry and the work of all the arts. Then what is made with hands—after all, so small a part of life—will have for model what is created and continually recreated, and the social being of a man will be able to move freely in humanity, going from strength to strength as it finds its way from the home to the school, from the school to the factory, from the factory to the various councils of men, sharing in communal pleasures and arts, and learning from them the skill to guard and preserve its private joys. Confronted with union for good the powers of evil would then be dissipated and distracted, for separation is evil's opportunity, unity its despair. The kingdom of God that is within men would then find this earth a place in which it could give forth its authority, and men would be able to communicate with each other fully: no longer in the bastard tongue of the market place, but with the fully uttered thought that needs sanction before it can appear upon the lips or in the eyes to illuminate the countenance. Who that has ever loved, or has found himself saluted by book, song, painting, or sculpture, or almost intolerably moved by dramatic speech, does not know the joy of seeing faces become countenances? There is no greater source of misery than seeing day by day faces that cannot kindle, faces that neither give nor reflect any light and are but masks to cover suffering. So prevalent is this misery that it would seem that society also is but a mask to cover the wretchedness of humanity, a screen set up between the human conscience and the doings of men; and it is to maintain this that the work of the world is perverted. Yet men work to defend themselves against the ills of life. Why, then, do they so aggravate them?

The answer to that question provides some illumination.

The world on which we live is round, and every community in it is a segment of a circle.

The work of every community moves towards the centre, but, with the exception of the work of the artists, is never suffered to pass through the centre into the other segments. Instead, it is carried laboriously round the circumference, because work is confused with the commodities produced by it. But the most important result of work is credit, and that is as easily transferable as any other mental or spiritual thing. Credit is held up at the centre of the circle, with the result that the vast majority of human beings in every segment, every community, are deprived of credit and the release it should give from anxiety. No one segment can exist without the other, no community can live apart from the whole, and yet each uses its credit against the other and deprives its members of the credit of the whole. The divorce of man from humanity is repeated in the financial system of the world. Each community regards its credit as something distinct from the credit created by the individuals composing it; that is to say, the community, which should be the conduit of credit from man to humanity and from humanity to man, usurps and abuses it, and until that is remedied there cannot be the liberty or the leisure or the enthusiasm necessary for social architecture, because the great mass of men have to work for an inadequate return and are cheated of their just share in the life of the community which can only be imparted to them first of all in credit. That granted, the rest follows. For a man to be able to contribute more than his bare labour to the community he must be given his due share of credit, and no longer asked to consent in its being wasted in the luxury of bellicose patriotism and the vain attempt to make commercial competition do the work of co-operation. All that has been aggravated by the rapid improvement of transport, but the mania for speed that blinds the Europeans of this century is a joke to those who know the speed of the spirit and the incomparable flight of the imagination. The speeding-up of production so dear to Americans can only aggravate the present congestion of credit, unless means are taken to see to it that the credit accorded to a nation benefits the individuals in it; and this can only be done by the removal of a class whose function is the manipulation of credit, which they do irresponsibly and the more ineffectively as the enormous accumulations of credit in a great modern community are apt to intoxicate the minds of those who are in a position uncontrolled to dispose of them. Every man for a week's work should be in a position to guarantee his livelihood for the following week, and with every week's work to increase his guarantee, the risk of his dying being borne by the community as part of his credit, the community in the first place having accepted the risk of his being born. To arrange this it must become as impossible for a man to set his nation above humanity as for him to set his family above his nation, but with the release of credit this would come about in the nature of things, for the incentive to set a smaller loyalty above the greater would disappear. Equality of rights would then only be tempered by a grading of duties, and that would automatically adjust itself, for the higher a duty and the more noble its performance the less does a man seek to be rewarded for it.

Credit is already centralised, but it is disposed of at the caprice of men whose sole idea of serving humanity is to show a profit, even at the cost of human suffering. Establish control of credit and the necessity for maintaining it by nefarious means disappears. The science of accountancy can replace the blundering methods of Finance, which at present only allow accountancy to disclose a profit, and not to provide a means by which credit can be transferred from the community to the working individual.

When the individual has been given his credit—the most direct way of making him feel his oneness with humanity—he must be educated to know how to use it, both as producer and as consumer, and as a member of the various groups to which he is attached, the family, the industrial group, the municipality, the nation, the community, each group being in the position of trustee to its subordinate, taking work from it and giving it credit in return. This social structure is already beginning to appear. The spirit with which it shall be animated has been preserved against all usurping authorities by the great democracy of the artists and scientists, between whom and suffering humanity remains only the bankrupt system of finance which is the fatal legacy of feudalism, with its pernicious system of privileges (a rudimentary form of credit) and monopolies. The disappearance of royal dynasties has left in power innumerable dynasties, respectable and propertied families who maintain their ascendancy exactly as royal personages used to do by supporting armed forces and laws which enslave the workers to their property. To protect themselves against the organisation of the workers they have been driven into international combination, in spite of their fervent protests of nationalism; and in this way have created the great pool of the world's credit that has at last brought its healthy circulation within the bounds of possibility. As the transport of commodities is facilitated the transference of credit must be made even more expeditious, and the necessary readjustment is impeded by the waste of credit upon national defences which for a long time now have in fact been merely an excuse by which the propertied dynasties maintained their control of credit. They were forced to frighten the ignorant masses into acquiescence, but the use of fear as an instrument of government is a boomerang, because it rouses the animal impulses in great herds of men, and these, once roused, will be satisfied. Those who cannot govern except through fear prove their unfitness for it.

Men as individuals have learned that it does

not pay to be governed by their appetites. Men in society have yet to learn that the same laws apply to humanity as a whole, and that humanity, like themselves, must be governed by the mind, as, indeed, unconsciously it is. The time is coming when they may be conscious. The appetites of men are unruly. Thwarted in the lives of individual men, they break loose in society, provoking sporadic outbursts of revolt against the government of the mind. The tyrants and conquerors of the world have ruined themselves by leading that revolt: the Cæsars, the Cromwells, the Napoleons; but they and their works are broken on the will of humanity, which does not operate through violence and sudden convulsions, but by the slow, inexorable force of vision seeking expression in form. The true leaders of men are the visionaries, but they lead at a distance of generations. The visible and immediate leaders are, or should be, those who have been kindled by the vision into honesty, so that it is their concern to preserve it from the rebellious appetites of men, and they would no more exploit the appetite for wealth than they would that for food or women or indecency. With some, even a slight element of form introduced into society, men would as naturally follow their true leaders as they have learned to obey the law, and as social beings they would as gladly accept the mind's ordering of the appetites as they do in their individual lives. It is certain that civilised men cannot much longer accept the barbaric dictates of the community, or respond to the base appeals made to their appetites by the dynasties for whom their profoundest needs are sacrificed. If men are granted their due of credit and liberty they can be trusted to abide by the social contract. If, on the other hand, they are forced into a sullen acquiescence it will not be long before their appetites, always in revolt against the mind, will leap to the revolt in their souls, take fire from it and drive them out upon errands of destruction.

The horror of the war of 1914-18 is the measure of the social injustice from which it sprang. The fact that no great tyrant or conqueror has come out of it is the measure of the extent to which the social conscience and the feeling for social structure have been released by it. The appetites seek the leadership of an ambitious man: the mind pursues rather the guidance of the spirit. Out of the tragedy has come no great human figure, but in the humblest heart the spirit is felt at work; the desire to make of this earth not a brawling place of the passions, but a most holy abiding place where those passions can be turned to noble uses and to the creation of a life where men and women can live together, not in that peace which is a mere folding of the hands, but in the peace which is a striving after more and more delight, that no moment of joy or suffering, of suffering through joy, and of joy through suffering, may escape unlived. That can only be if men leave their primitive and beaver-like building of dams, and will, on the high ground conquered for them by the visionaries, build and rebuild, even as Nature builds her seasons, a house whose flooring is the human heart and whose roof is the firmament, whence light comes to call into men's eyes the tender and more penetrating light of the soul. For the house is not to be built with hands, and only by that light can the materials for it be chosen.

IX

EAST AND WEST

IX

EAST AND WEST

The mystics of the East sink into their contemplation the more directly to commune with the will of humanity. Escaping the brawling noise of every day they can through the silence hear the murmuring of truth, and in silence release it to pass into the turbulence of men and women to sweeten it and to keep them from perishing. And the East accepts that these are holy men and prizes their function in society, even relies on it too much, and acquiesces in the scourges of life—poverty, disease, famine—against which the West these hundreds of years has been in revolt. Because the mystic cannot stay these scourges he is in the West ignored because his function is not understood, and in the West men imagine that it is better to perish of untruth than of plague. In the struggle against physical afflictions spiritual distempers are ignored, though it is worse for herds of men to perish in mid-life than to be swept away by some raging pestilence, because the harm done to humanity by the morally dead is infinitely worse than that which is done by the actively evil, for this is a flame that burns itself out while that is a smouldering and creeping fire. In all its plagues, famines, poverty and disease the East is far in advance of the West in moral understanding, and can afford to smile at the Occidentals with their irrigation, sanitation, railways, canals, aeroplanes and steamships. These the East can accept and assimilate, without disturbing its traditions, while waiting for the West to understand the meaning of silence and the importance of the distinction between time and eternity. The difference arises from taking up the stick at different ends. The East approaches the mystery of being from what we, following Wordsworth, have called intimations of immortality, while the West attacks rather than approaches it from the phenomena of existence which it elects to call life.

The admission of the single community of humanity brings East and West together without a clash. There may be war between the yellow races and the white, but it will assuredly not be a war over their differences but a matter of commercial advantage; and it can only come through the indecent haste of the Occidentals, or it may only come through the final refusal of the propertied dynasties of the West—enthroned in Anglo-Saxon suburbs—to surrender their monopoly of credit. All that remains to be seen, but the evolution of society has gone so far that war has lost any significance it ever had, and is henceforth to be classed with the traffic in prostitutes, opium, alcohol and pornographic literature and photographs as an evil to be stamped out. If the West is to instruct the East in physical well-being, the East has to tutor the West in spiritual and in the art of practising religion, and of the two the West has the easier task. A nation in these days can become industrialised in a generation, but, as the English have so painfully shown, it is by far not enough to be industrialised. Much that was precious in the older and slowly grown civilisations has to be reconstituted. Traditions seem to disappear in the fever of increased production—and with that of multiplied population—but they remain untouched and bide their time. The English tradition that has seemed to be suspended after the Napoleonic wars found its isolated souls, a Gissing, a Mark Rutherford, in which, however faintly, to express itself. The true tradition of a race is not in those achievements recorded by history, but in its utterance of truth. That is its real contribution to civilisation, and all else follows directly or indirectly in its train. The English tradition is for quietude and order against which the robust appetites of the English have always been in revolt, just as the ferocious appetites of the French have always been in revolt against their logical genius. There are three logics: that of the spirit, that of the mind, and that of the heart—the first is Eastern, the second French, the third English. The Russians, in whom the great drama of East and West is being played, are attempting to reconcile all three. That is the significance and the importance to humanity of the Russian Revolution. Without logic there can be no social structure. The French Revolution pursued the logic of the mind: that is not enough. The English Revolution pursued the logic of the heart: that is not enough. Nor, by itself, is the logic of the spirit enough. Religion has symbolised these three in the Trinity, and that is the symbol to which the Russian Revolution is attempting to restore validity, though its force has been diverted to the establishment of communist economic theories in order to checkmate the operations of European and American capitalism. Russia, half-Asiatic, is bound to defend itself against the vices of civilisation, even at the cost of anarchy and famine. It is a case in which the beggar cannot without dishonour accept aid from the rich man. Russia, indeed, stands for the revolt of humanity against the rich, who have forced that rebellion by their refusal to admit that they hold their riches upon trust. Centuries ago the Christian Religion was split on this very point, and the Byzantine Church retained more of the mystic quality of the teaching of Jesus than did the Roman.

Mysticism implies an intensification of life, not an escape from it. The East has understood this, while the West, crude enough to be in a hurry even in its hope of Heaven, has degraded religion to the level of a syrup for weariness of the soul, with the result that the logic of the mind has been fanatically pursued in Europe to end in a social theory by which human nature is repelled. This mood of repulsion, dragging through generations, has given the materially minded the opportunity which they have not been slow to use, and they have developed and organised the commercial side of international intercourse, but no other, and life which should have been intensified has been relaxed. With greater opportunities for life than their predecessors, men in the modern world live less, and are more fatally unable to rise to the height of a great occasion. Great communities crumble into desuetude out of sheer physical and mental inanition. They have lost the thread of the logic of the spirit largely because under modern organisation men and women live too much in public. The monotony of daily and excessive toil has reduced them to a dull uniformity of shallow thoughts and superficial emotions. A sophisticated life has been established in the West without achieving the simplicity which is the object of sophistication. The problem is, as always, how to preserve in society the natural and beautiful simplicity of Man, which, if it be assailed, he is ferocious to defend. A society that knows only political and economic aims is injurious to that simplicity, and creates, as we have seen during the nineteenth century with its tragic climax, a growing sullen discontent, a blind animosity, a feverish jealousy. Such a society sophisticates, but deadens and disappoints the soul. It creates millions of characterless beings, whose dullness creeps into the institutions they labour to support; and these, for lack of sustaining vitality, crash under the strain put upon them. When an institution becomes a burden to the people for whom it has been evolved it must be destroyed, and it is not always desirable that it should be replaced. There is always the possibility that they may have outgrown the need for it. . . . It certainly looks as though men in the East had long outgrown institutions that the Occidentals are still bloodily fighting to preserve. In China, at any rate, men have achieved what has never been done in the West, save by a few rare individuals—that simplicity, through sophistication, which is not superhuman, but is simply human nature released from its cramping obsessions and perplexing passions and taking the integrity of the soul as a matter of course, and no more to be disputed than the act of breathing or seeing or loving. A Chinese poet can understand liberty, while a Western poet can only be lyrical or rhetorical about it. Between the two there is the difference between adolescence and manhood, and that is the difference that has to be spanned between the East and the West. The boyish adventurers of Europe have lived by robbing the world's orchards, lustily imagining that they were opening up Eldorado, only to find that there are men in the East who know more of life and the world than they, without even troubling to cross their thresholds. Disconcerting to Western ideas though the simplicity of the peasant and the savage have always been, it can be and has been answered with the machine-gun, but that is a sorry weapon against the simplicity of sophistication, which is a purely aristocratic state, inimical only to vulgarity and mediocrity, and not at all to the spirit of democracy. Because that simplicity is known in the East more than in the West, it is likely that democracy will be established there sooner than in Europe and America; because the issues will be less confused and the desirable thing, a democracy of aristocrats, is discernible as it is not in conditions perturbed by war, revolution and industrial feuds. In a time of stress simplification is the only outlet, and those survive best who do not allow any idea or any emotion to usurp the sovereignty of the soul. They alone can see whither they are going, the dangers that have to be met, the risks that must be taken, and they waste no energy in arguing or wrangling or in thwarting others. They alone can recognise an event before it takes shape in life, and are therefore in a position to combine with their fellows to meet it. This power of foresight and combination is of the essence of policy, and without it there can be no guidance: but without the swift logic of the spirit it is impossible. Even intuition is not enough, for without the vision the logics of the mind and the heart are without premises, they can reach no precise conclusions, and are often driven into action before the occasion is ripe for it or the probable outcome is discernible. The wise man, the wise nation, knows that the course of events is decided long before human responsibility arises, and that nothing can alter it, though human action can interfere with its effect upon human affairs, and the relations, happy or unhappy, of men with each other and with the rest of creation. The happiness of men and women depends entirely upon the degree of their understanding, which is therefore the only thing to be desired. A state of society which stultifies understanding must be amended, or, if it is too rigid for that, then destroyed. When civilisation is perverted and understanding is corrupt, then even the keenest intelligence is impotent to save the wretched peoples from disaster. To this is attributable the present helplessness of the European nations. At no time can the level of intelligence have been so high, knowledge so widely spread, information so readily available, methods of communication so adequate, and yet for lack of understanding there is no co-ordination of these advantages or power to turn them to the use of all. Russia, on the threshold of industrial civilisation, refuses to enter it for this reason. Russia cannot divorce herself from the East, and the West cannot afford to abandon her, and therefore Russia insists that in the soul of her race East and West shall meet to reconcile the simple, inactive, aristocratic spirit with the seething turbulent spirit of democracy. It is not a question of choosing the always ruinous middle way, but of the meeting of extremes, that aristocracy may learn its purpose, and democracy the meaning of the rights it clamours for so vociferously and so vainly. To achieve this it is necessary for the European races to admit that they have common interests and passions higher than those of war. It is upon this that Russia is insisting, asserting her will and vision against the organised military and economic power of the Allies in whom neither will nor vision appear. Once more in an acute form has arisen the deadlock between East and West that they have no common terms in which to meet. Will can speak to will, vision can signal to vision, but what has will to say to economic power, and how should military force see vision? The West calls economic and military organisation democracy, but the East knows that it is only machinery, more than half of which is unnecessary and wasteful, and the East, through Russia, demands the sacrifice of it before entering into the common effort for the deliverance of humanity from the scourges that now inflict it. With railways and steamships it should be easy to avert famine; with medicine and scientific hygiene it should be possible to stamp out epidemic plagues; with a communal spirit it should be within the power of the present generation to rid the world of war, and the East, through Russia, calls on the West to co-operate. If the barbarians of Europe can learn anything at all they should have learned it by now, and if they are capable of consummating the Revolution begun in 1789 they can hardly set about it too soon. Unable for a century to find spiritual confidence they have accepted material security as a stop-gap only to find it intolerable. They know that civilisation is possible, that it has been achieved by humanity, for the soul of man is one and yields up its secrets to the suffering, and they know also that civilisation is not an end but a means. To regard it as an end is to enthrone mediocrity, to achieve stagnation and through that corruption. France, England, Germany, Italy, America have all achieved the stagnation of mediocrity which Russia, in the name of the East, and of humanity, refuses to accept, because it is a worse state than barbarism; being, indeed, barbarism intensified by the arts of combination, for the mediocre in their insensible complacency deny the only two real virtues, the simplicity of the primitive and the simplicity of the sophisticated, and abhor logic of any kind, preferring to drift and to fight if necessary to preserve the illusion of security they have set up as their sole aim and end. That illusion is the chief impediment in the way of the healthy growth of civilisation. The

Europeans have been imprisoned in it for so long, that even though it is now possible for them to escape from it they cannot seize their opportunity; and when they use phrases like "making the world safe for democracy" can only interpret them as meaning that they must admit the rest of humanity to their prison, which is the very last thing that the rest of humanity desires. It is true, of course, that the only security lies in democracy, but democracy is a far greater and a far more simple thing than the economic and military organisation which the Western nations are pleased to call by that name. Democracy is organised goodwill, and it is not to be achieved by the methods of hatred, jealousy, cupidity and exploitation. These can lead to the success of the adventurous and the bold in a community, but not to the well-being of the community, without which any success is barren, because, though a community may throw up great men, they can do nothing if they are urged solely in the direction of economic or military conquest. Marcus Aurelius could not save the Roman Empire from decay.

The movements which restore the health of humanity come from the people. It is only after a generation or two that they find clear expression in great men whose vision is towards the next great movement. There is a confused migration, an interpenetration, much suffering and great tragedy as the weak are swallowed up in the effort of the strong. Leaders of groups appear and disappear, groups form and break, powers burst and authorities crack like old walls against the pressure of growing trees. For a while men can live on their inheritance from the past. When that is exhausted they can sustain themselves with the intoxication of living for the future, but in the end they are brought to the inexorable fact that their duty is to the present. Then slowly order returns: new communities are formed on the ruins of the old, but with a new interfusion of the races and a more realistic geographical sense. The people, it seems, have to learn in a hard practical way what their visionaries have always told them. The generation in which such a movement comes learns as much as it can digest and settles down to work and brood on its lesson, and impatient and practical people want quick results. The generations are jealous of each other, and one cannot to another communicate its wisdom directly; but all is carried on the deep stream of humanity from which all life comes, to return again enriched by consciousness. It is idle, then, to look to any system of government for social perfection. That system is best which allows the greatest freedom of movement to the human spirit. The Eastern races seem to have learned that long ago, but the wisdom of the East is only just beginning to dawn upon the West, where the spirit of anarchy has again and again destroyed tradition, and brought ruin to civilisations that imagined themselves to be at their zenith, forgetful that the barbarism most to be dreaded was in themselves. A civilisation which takes too much from the work of the masses who sustain it without giving them the due return of slowly increasing liberty cannot endure. The people wither away and the foundations crumble. No amount of material wealth can then stave off a collapse.

Very pathetic, then, is the attempt of the great nations of the West to avert disaster by increasing power and diminishing liberty. Only the release of human energy can restore the vanished health of the people, but it is still proposed to waste and confine that energy in military effort, by which it is designed to ward off the danger threatened from visionary Russia. Behind Russia is the East, where affairs are dominated by the logic of the spirit, the very instrument that is needed in the West. Because Russia will not and cannot relinquish it, the Russian people are starving and suffering the agonies of civil war. They need also the two logics evolved in the West, but, viewing the West with clear-sighted eyes, they cannot accept them as sufficient; and also as this stupendous drama is being played out in their souls they are aware of their responsibility to humanity and will not betray it, preferring to sink into the very pit of chaos, and, if need be, to begin again at the beginning. No race can accept as right the grim grey dullness and uniformity of the British proletariat. No race in the name of humanity can admit that such is the just and inevitable price of industrialism. Revolution in Russia and Germany is the assertion of that truth. Let us be clear about that. The revolution in Eastern Europe is not merely a political upheaval and a reorganisation of the communities of the three Emperors, it is an emphatic repudiation of the materialism of the West, a protest against the formation of the single community necessitated by the machinery of modern commerce to be dominated by commercial calculations, and a vehement declaration that life for the community as for the individual begins where commerce ends.

The human spirit may for a time seem impotent against the economic power of the "Big Five," with their control of raw materials, but that power maintains its monopoly at the cost of repudiating both the aristocratic and the democratic impulses of that spirit which in consequence does not enter into its operations at all, and without it they achieve nothing but a fevered movement without direction or purpose. The British attempt to compromise at material security has led only to an upheaval of those very forces of barbarism and crude appetite which it sought to avoid. At the same time the compromise has given men certain powers over the old limitations of existence, without which the single community cannot become an actuality to the human consciousness. Community of material interests leads to spiritual interpenetration, which by divergence of such interests is distracted and impeded. The blunder that is being committed lies in imagining that the single community has to be created. It exists. It has always existed. The sufferings of men have arisen from the refusal of the component communities to acknowledge it, and that refusal has arisen largely from the lack of effective means of communication. Those have been established, but so ingrained is the piratical habit of the powerful among men that they have been seized as a means of holding recalcitrant communities to ransom. Individuals in the modern world are practically immune from robbery, because it is so much easier to plunder communities. This can be done with impunity, because it is authorised by the laws made and handed down by the robbers of old times. The Big Five in the League of Nations are simply holding up the rest of the world, particularly the East, to force it to accept unmitigated industrialism. The answer of the remaining communities is democracy, for which they, having long passed the elementary stage in which commercial adventure seems the highest possible advance on piracy, are ripe. All the world except the Big Five is ready to admit the existence of the single community. The Big Five, confused with war and warlike conceptions, vainly imagine that the single community is waiting for them to create it. The Big Five are against, the rest of the world is for, humanity. In the long run that which *is* prevails against that which, however splendidly, appears to be.

X

DEMOCRACY

X

DEMOCRACY

Democracy is not a form of government, it *is* government. Every other system is either a tyranny or a veiled form of anarchy. Only under democracy can the realities of existence be dealt with and turned to the service of mankind. Every other attempted government must deal with illusions. Admitting that government depends upon discipline, the only true discipline is self-discipline. If the possibility of that be removed, whatever appearance may be maintained, beneath it there can only be chaos.

A traveller journeying through that country which is most proud of being democratic, Great Britain, would perceive the impossibility of acknowledging the claim as he saw the huddled streets and houses in which for the most part the people live. He would know the impossibility of self-discipline in people denied beauty, air, health, privacy, social intercourse, civic pride; and condemned from week to week to a monotony of toil by which they are drilled into the uniformity of subservience. Much the same impression would be given one who should journey round the environs of Paris or take a trip by train across the industrial area of Belgium. What Verhaeren called the tentacular town sucks men in from the earth, gives them a new consciousness, but robs them of the vitality to use it; and government in the West depends entirely upon the linking up of these tentacular towns and the reduction of their populations to uniformity, so that they will in blind obedience acquiesce in the operations of those who, by intrigue, have gained control of the machinery of communication. A man lunching in the Midland Hotel, Manchester, or the Carlton at Johannesburg, can perceive no essential difference in his surroundings, and it makes no difference to him whether he buys furniture from Maple's in Tottenham Court Road or Maple's in Buenos Aires. Poor man or rich, white, yellow, brown or black, whatever energy he puts forth contributes to the growth of the tentacular towns and accelerates the means of communication between them. So far as the exchange of commodities is concerned internationalisation is complete, and it is characterless because it has been hastily accomplished at the cost of devitalising the proletariat. The invading Germans destroyed the Cloth Hall at Ypres, but they left intact the tentacular town of Lille.

There will be, there almost is, a world-chain of such towns, providing a method so vastly more expeditious of exchanging commodities and transferring work from one community to another that all others are demoded. What, then, was it that necessitated the sacrifice of so many millions of lives and the collapse of the greater part of Europe into famine and anarchy? Partly the discomfort of being deprived of old traditions, partly inability to shake off the remnants of patriarchal conceptions, but chiefly the mental confusion which imagined democracy to be a matter of the ballot, a purely political thing which admitted some element of reason into human affairs, but denied the operation of the conscience. The pressure of the industrial upon the political centres of the world had become intolerable, and the close bureaucratic power of London, Paris and Berlin had to be broken. To save themselves they opened the sluice-gates and let the industrial forces of Europe spend themselves in the wasteful effort of the war. Berlin, with its alcove St. Petersburg, has been swept away, but London and Paris, linked now with New York, remain. The industrial centres will once more gather up their forces, only to have them checked and impeded by the new political group, which refuses to admit that democracy is more than a political system. To the pressure of steam power has been added that of electricity and oil, but the political group, as insensible to industrial pressure as to any kind of spiritual vision, takes the victory over Berlin as evidence of the rightness of its attitude, and refuses to amend or jettison a single one of its ideas. But the collapse of Berlin and St. Petersburg is not the victory of Paris, London and New York, it is the victory of industrialism fighting for democracy, and the first to reap its fruits will be the Germans and the Russians, who will become reconciled to the spirit of the East, while the Allied Nations will be still sullenly insurgent against political tyranny, wasting their efforts in the maintenance of armaments to defend ideas which have lost their validity. The removal of Berlin by itself means an immense saving of money to the German people and a vast gain in responsibility for their industrial centres, already far in advance of the British in self-government. If the world-community is to take shape in a series of tentacular towns linked together with railways, roads and air-routes, its health must depend upon the ease with which those towns can co-operate and respond to each others' needs. Administrative areas then will be determined by geography and not by race, by railways and ports and not by strategic considerations. Military ideas are maintained in London, Paris and New York (and possibly in Tokyo) entirely to serve the vested interests that have grown up round them, but the great industrial centres are of far more importance to society than the capitals, and these military ideas have lost their roots. The ideas that shall replace them have hardly begun to show above the surface, and the unhappy masses of humanity huddled together in the towns can only move by instinct, which at present bids them to go on working if only to avoid thinking. How, lacking ideas, can they think? They can only keep the machines running and trust to collective impulse to keep them from an insane revolt and a ruinous breach in the circulation of work upon which their lives depend. They know the vastness of the power they have created, and they know the feebleness of the hands in which it rests. They know, too, that they must take the control into their own hands. But to do that they must have a common centre, a common law which all will obey, and a responsible executive. Rights and privileges from top to bottom of society must conform to duties, but to achieve all the nice adjustments necessary there must be rest from the daily drudgery of tending the machine, and there must be relief from the pressure of the tentacular towns, which must be rebuilt to let in air, the healing and creative work of Nature, beauty, form and proportion. The linking together of the towns gives the power and the wealth to remedy their disastrous influence, but it is taken and frittered away by the political centres maintaining useless and injurious forms of government, though the proletariat of the world knows in its heart that there are no forms of government, that there is only Government, and that Government is democracy, which alone admits of the application of the aristocratic principle, the rule of the best; for only democracy can liberate conscience, the power to choose between good and evil, and of the good to choose the best. Government in the past has depended upon the obliteration of conscience, either through open slavery, or by the threat of poverty, or in the rudimentary stage of industrialism by State education, which substitutes rough-and-ready instruction in certain ideas and conduct for the delicate process of nurturing the minds of children through the difficult years of the ripening of conscience. The rudimentary stages of industrialism are long past. The system can now be assimilated by a community without paying the heavy price that the Europeans have paid for it. The economic restoration of the devastated countries is a comparatively simple matter. The terrible problem is how to repair the poverty of spirit of the leaders in industrialism. Must they, too, be brought to ruin before they can understand? Inertia, stagnation, indifference, are deadlier than famine and pestilence. When neither joy nor suffering can stir the hearts of the people the spirit cannot move among them, and their days are separate one from another, their lives are isolated and nothing can unite them. They are impervious to the achievement of the past and can hand on nothing to the future. They remain dull, stationary, parasitic upon humanity, which at last discards them and their works.

Democracy is government by faith, and for lack of faith it is not attempted, though the state of the world, even the physical discomfort of the people, cry out that it should be admitted. Trotsky at Brest-Litovsk, Eisner at Berne, Wilson in Paris, have all laid it down as the inevitable form of society to which the nations must submit; but unhappily France, England and America, all communities suffering under the tyranny of economic power, believe themselves to be democratic, and, indignant that other communities do not see eye to eye with them, denounce them as anarchic, refuse to treat with them, starve them, deprive them of trade and the opportunity of trading. It is precisely their use of economic power that proves them undemocratic, but to this they are blind. Their spokesmen are eloquent in praise of democracy, but qualify it with nationalism. But qualified democracy is nothing. As well speak of qualified poetry. The spirit of democracy, like that of poetry, can be coloured but not confined by nationality.

The politicians of the victorious Allies are like a man standing on his hose-pipe and cursing everybody in his garden because no water is forthcoming. It is his own foot that wants removing.

Unfortunately, however, the greater the urgency of the need for admitting that a change has come about, the stiffer the obstinacy with which it is refused. The fight of the manufacturers against the landed aristocracy is a small thing compared with that of the proletariat against the manufacturers clinging to the antiquated methods of government of the aristocracy. Such methods are lavish and recklessly expensive, and the proletariat very properly wants to know why the laws of economy should not apply to them, since their immunity makes those laws too stringent in their application to domestic life. The manufacturers also wanted to know this while they were fighting, but directly the fight was over they adopted for their business corporations the immorality which had been the privilege of the powerful political combinations which conducted, or misconducted, the affairs of humanity. Uncontrolled power is corrosive, and it has been proved by bitter experience that political control by means of the vote does not provide a sufficient check, and indeed has only aggravated power by making it possible for rulers to throw responsibility on to the ruled. Acting only through political machinery, public opinion cannot be brought into operation swiftly enough, because without connecting machinery the minds of the people cannot link political cause with industrial and domestic effect. They realise the connection in time, but always too late. Parliamentary institutions could exercise some control over the economic power of a landed aristocracy, but without democratic control in industry they are impotent in the face of that of manufacturers and undertakers, who, operating internationally, can present a national Parliament with an accomplished fact and leave it to placate its electors as best it can. An international Parliament is now a necessity, but by itself can only aggravate the evils of the capitalistic system. It can only function properly if it is made democratic by devolution and the fusion of political and industrial institutions. Otherwise the increasing pressure of industrialism, acting as a blind and undirected force, will crash its way through to achieve in the end hideously and destructively what might be accomplished patiently with foresight and enthusiasm—the reconstruction of society to conform outwardly to what in essence it is: Democracy.

There is much of the past that it is desirable to preserve—the slowly developed instinctive observance of order, the social sense, care for good manners, traditions of scholarship and urbanity. Refusal to yield to the pressure of industrialism and the crying needs of the proletariat can only mean the destruction of the good with the bad and the reduction of society to the bare machinery of existence, a means of providing food, clothes and shelter. But humanity is so constituted that without the quality of ecstasy it cannot even fulfil efficiently its rudimentary functions. Ecstasy is the moving force of evolution, the breaking of the chrysalis into the butterfly. Without it life is aimless and intolerably hideous. In the deadlock that has arisen between political and industrial institutions human beings everywhere are being starved of ecstasy. The dragging misery of life creates in every individual a hard shell that makes him impervious to every other. Ecstasy lives in the soul of humanity, but not in the single separate soul of the individual to whom it is communicated through the love of his fellows. It is the creeping tragedy of modern life that the powers of love in men and women are denied their sustenance from the soul of humanity, because they are cramped and stifled in communities engaged in a deadly and futile rivalry that ends in mutual destruction, when they should be joined together in the sole aim of achieving mutual elevation.

Change is so slow as to be hardly perceptible, but there are times when its accumulated effect has to be admitted and dealt with consciously. Slow though change may be, it is swifter than the minds of men who invent tools, engines and social machinery to overtake it and never quite succeed. Increasing consciousness of change has produced a frenzy of invention, and still men lag behind because they have not yet learned that the world they live in is a spiritual structure, a soul in which an infinite number of souls are built together, that life and death are but architectonic principles, and that the great building of the soul is contained in and inspired with infinite love.

In this great building, blind to its majestic beauty, they huddle into corners, creep away from the light, defile and abuse themselves and each other, and every now and then bring themselves to such a pitch of misery that they must move, must come into the light, must see the light in each other's eyes, and thereby something of the beauty amid which they are privileged to dwell. They perceive form and colour, and they desire them above all things for the ecstasy they bring, and in that ecstasy a new age is born. The remnants of the old are cast away, and for a space they can live freely in accordance with perceived design: the various elements of their existence fall into their places and are locked together to give them the energy with which to live, and to explore the soul of humanity from which comes wealth indivisible and inexhaustible.

> Love in this differs from gold and clay
> That to divide is not to take away.

The great effort of the early years of the nineteenth century was not in vain, though for so long it has seemed to be thwarted into sterility. The practical sense of humanity, knowing what rare treasure was unearthed, set about to reorganise society, that this treasure might admit ecstasy to the life of every day when at last drudgery could be kindled into work.

For that it was necessary to break down barriers, the beaver-dams that men had built against the rich waters of the creative will; it was necessary to destroy old faiths, old systems, immemorial habits. Men became a race of rodents, gnawing away until the house they dwelt in came tumbling about their ears. It was necessary for them to be banded together in a stern monotony of toil; but it is necessary no longer, because the destructive labours to which they were committed are at an end, ceased indeed a generation ago. Destruction is best wrought in separation: for it is grim work, only to be wrought with a fixed will, holding in abeyance the fluid and infinitely supple creative will of humanity. For men living as they should there should never be any necessity for a will so fixed. It is forced on them by the indolence of the generations, for when the creative will is admitted to human activity it brings destruction with its creation exactly as it does in Nature. In the long process of sophistication men lose the wisdom that they share with birds and beasts and trees.

They cannot rest content with unconscious wisdom, for it brings no sufficient ecstasy. Men must be conscious.

At long last and after generations of tragedy they have achieved that. The revelation of its possibility passes from soul to soul, East and West, and to make ready for it the great common life of democracy is prepared. Society is explored, understood, charted exactly as the earth has been: its barriers and checks and injurious controls are removed, and conscious men everywhere begin to demand the right to exercise their conscience in everything they do, in their public and in their private lives, that the ecstasy without which life is a bitter confinement of the spirit may freely move from soul to soul, and from heart to heart.

No power, no interest, can resist this growing impulse which will have society reconstituted in accordance with its structure and with universal law. The petty laws of expediency of the various communities that have been and are so reluctant to relinquish their selfishness will break before it like ice in the spring thaw; for this impulse has given men a new knowledge. The scientific discovery of fact is not enough for them. They know now that no fact is discovered until it shines as a symbol, and except with shining symbols they will not build. It is for this that the grey-faced proletariat is waiting. Unscrupulous men may act on dull and unrelated facts to their apparent profit and real hurt, but men in the mass can only move, can only act under inspiration. They have now the impulse towards democracy, but no vision of it, because democracy can only be won by men when Man to them becomes a symbol of the God who lives in every moment of life. Man for men is the key symbol, the solvent of the facts that have been unearthed by science. With the use of that symbol facts can be related, and their validity can be tested. Those that shine as symbols can be used for action, while those that remain dead and dull can be rejected as half-truths or mistaken conclusions. Man, with all his varied powers, his desires, passions and the three logics of his being, spirit, mind and heart, is a democracy governed by the aristocratic principle, his conscience, which selects his best and noblest, and keys his forces and capacities up to that, and in the fullness of time Man cannot but make Society in his own image.

Date Due
